KEN[T]

YEAR ROUND WALKS

Spring, Summer, Autumn & Winter

Michael Easterbrook

COUNTRYSIDE BOOKS
NEWBURY BERKSHIRE

Countryside Books
3 Catherine Road
Newbury
Berkshire
RG14 7NA

To view our complete range of books please visit us at
www.countrysidebooks.co.uk

First published 2015
Reprinted 2016, 2019
Text © 2015 Michael Easterbrook

A CIP record for this book is available from the British Library.

ISBN 978 1 84674 295 8

All materials used in the manufacture of this book carry FSC certification

Produced by The Letterworks Ltd., Reading
Typeset by KT Designs, St Helens
Printed by The Holywell Press, Oxford

Contents

Introduction

spring

Summer

Contents

Autumn

Winter

Introduction

The lovely countryside of Kent deserves to be appreciated at all times of the year and this book provides the opportunities to walk through its varied landscapes. In spring many of the woods have wonderful carpets of bluebells, plus other wild flowers such as wood anemones and celandines. Also, the orchards of fruit for which Kent is famous will be a froth of white and pink blossom. Summer sees the blooming of many flowers, including rare orchids, particularly on the chalk soils of the North Downs, and there are also colourful butterflies and dragonflies to be seen. In autumn the woods are burnished with shades of bronze and gold as the leaves change colour and there are splashes of red from the berries of holly and bryony. A crisp, sunny day in winter lends itself to a bracing walk, especially if it involves sea breezes. Many birds choose to overwinter in Kent and flocks of various species of ducks, geese and waders can be seen, particularly at the coast.

I have picked out some routes that will enable you to see all these aspects of the county and have suggested the most appropriate time of year to do each walk. However, I can recommend doing the walks at all times of year so that you can experience the changes in the countryside through the different seasons. Historic buildings are a permanent feature and I have drawn attention to the ancient houses, churches, castles and windmills that you can see on the walks.

You may feel like some refreshment at the end of your walk and I have mentioned pubs and tearooms that are close to the route. A sketch map accompanies each walk but it is a good idea to take the OS Explorer map for the region, as that will have more detail and will put the walk into the context of the wider area. I have suggested places to park but most of the walks are accessible by public transport. Timetables are available from train and bus companies. Some of the walks have slopes, mostly gradual but a few are quite steep and so a reasonable level of fitness is needed for those routes. There may be muddy patches after wet weather so suitable footwear is required. I hope you enjoy the walks and get a good experience from doing the routes at different times of the year.

Acknowledgements
I am grateful to David Chambers, and Cheryl and Justin Davenport-Thomas for their company on some of the walks. Photography on pages 91 and 92 by Adam Whitehouse.

Dedication
To Florence, our first grandchild – we hope you grow up to enjoy walking.

Michael Easterbrook

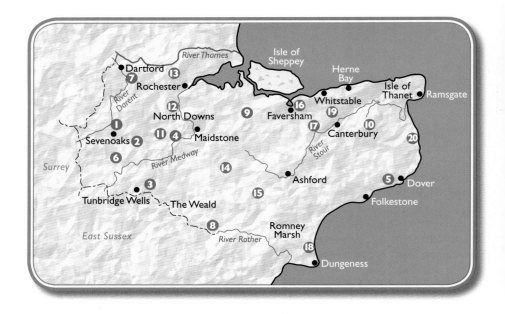

PUBLISHER'S NOTE

We hope that you obtain considerable enjoyment from this book; great care has been taken in its preparation. Although at the time of publication all routes followed public rights of way or permitted paths, diversion orders can be made and permissions withdrawn.

We cannot, of course, be held responsible for such diversion orders and any inaccuracies in the text which result from these or any other changes to the routes, nor any damage which might result from walkers trespassing on private property. We are anxious though that all the details covering the walks are kept up to date and would therefore welcome information from readers which would be relevant to future editions.

The simple sketch maps that accompany the walks in this book are based on notes made by the author whilst checking out the routes on the ground. They are designed to show you how to reach the start, to point out the main features of the overall circuit and they contain a progression of numbers that relate to the paragraphs of the text.

However, for the benefit of a proper map, we do recommend that you purchase the relevant Ordnance Survey sheet covering your walk. The Ordnance Survey maps are widely available, especially through booksellers and local newsagents.

1 Otford

Stunning views across the valley.

After an ascent from the picturesque village of Otford, with its lovely church, duck pond and remains of a bishop's palace, you are rewarded with glorious views over the Darent Valley. You pass through rolling countryside on the top of the downs, from where there are views to some of London's tallest buildings. You can see woods carpeted with bluebells in spring and colourful butterflies such as brimstone and orange-tip. The route comes down from the hills through majestic beech woods then returns along the valley.

Distance 6 miles.

Terrain Hilly, with some steep climbs and descents, one of which is down a long flight of steps.

Map OS Explorer 147 Sevenoaks & Tonbridge.

Starting point The car park in Otford village (GR 526594, TN14 5PQ).

How to get there Otford is 2 miles north of Sevenoaks. Turn off the A225 at the roundabout by the duck pond in the village to go west to the car park. Otford station is passed early on the walk.

Refreshments There is a selection of pubs and tearooms in Otford.

The Walk

❶ Turn left out of the entrance to the car park and walk alongside the main street, passing the duck pond and keeping straight on until you reach the railway station. Cross the road to the opposite pavement and continue over the bridge. As the main road bends left, turn right along **Pilgrims Way East**, signed to Kemsing.

❷ After 100 yards you reach a **North Downs Way** (NDW) fingerpost and information board. Cross the road with care and go up a brick-paved track opposite. The track climbs quite steeply between gardens then becomes a narrower path between fences before widening again as it climbs between trees. On reaching a welcome seat it is worth going through the bushes on the left for a few yards to gain a stunning view over the Darent valley. The walk continues straight ahead, to the right of the seat, going up steps and between bushes and trees such as yew and whitebeam. Continue through a wooden kissing gate and along the right edge of a field to a kissing gate in the far right corner.

❸ Go ahead with care across a narrow lane and a stony area with a signpost to another road on a bend. Continue ahead on this road, to the right of the sign for **Birchin Cross Road**. After 150 yards go right at a NDW fingerpost. After 20 yards the path bends sharp left between a wood on the right that is full of bluebells in spring and a meadow on the left. Continue ahead through three kissing gates, then alongside a wire fence on the right to reach a lane. Leave the NDW here by turning left on the lane to reach a T-junction. Turn left for 80 yards then right at a fingerpost onto a path between fences through **Great**

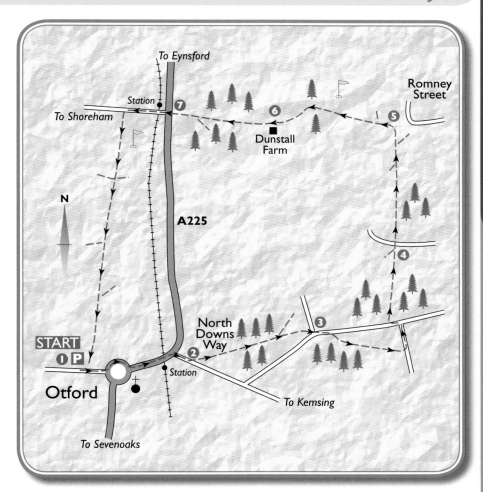

Wood. Leave the wood at a stile and go up a meadow to a stile next to a metal gate then ahead on the left side of a field. After 100 yards, at the corner of a fence on the left, keep straight on across the remainder of the field towards a gate at the end of a fence around a garden. Cross a stile next to the gate to reach a lane.

❹ Turn left for 20 yards then right at a fingerpost to go up through scrub to a stile, then along the left edge of a field to another, then ahead along the right edge of a long field, with a wood on the right. At the end of this field go over a stile to the left of a metal gate, then after 10 yards go through a metal pedestrian gate. Follow the path alongside a wire fence on the left, ignoring a path going

The rolling Darent valley has inspired many writers and artists.

off to the right. To the left ahead are far-reaching views to the River Thames, with Essex beyond, and to the tall buildings of Canary Wharf.

5 On reaching a T-junction with another path by a garden fence turn left to continue the walk. Go over a stile and ahead down a field with more views to the right. At the end of the field cross two stiles in quick succession then go carefully down the steep slope of a field along its right edge. At a stile with a golf warning notice go straight ahead on a wide path between overhanging bushes. Cross a tall stile then go up a slope that is colourful with chalkland flowers such as marjoram and knapweed, attracting meadow brown and common blue butterflies in summer. Go over a stile into a wood and follow the path as it winds between beech trees. Continue diagonally left (10 o'clock) across a field for 100 yards to a marker at the end of a fence by a large oak tree and maintain direction across the next field to reach a stony track. Go ahead on the track to reach **Dunstall Farm**.

6 Keep ahead across the farmyard for 100 yards then turn right by barns for 10 yards to go through a gateway by an information board about the cattle here. Turn sharp left alongside the barn to a short marker post then go straight ahead across a field towards a wood. Go on a path downhill through the wood, going straight over any cross-paths, and down a long flight of steps. Continue on the main path under majestic trees to a T-junction with another path and turn right for 300 yards to a main road.

7 Cross with great care to go along the road opposite, signed to **Shoreham** (the station is just to the right). Go past the entrance to a golf club and after 100 yards turn left at a fingerpost in trees. The path goes between fences through the golf course. Keep ahead to cross a fairway, being aware of any golfers hitting balls from the left, and keep to the left side of a cricket field. The path continues between fences and bushes. Go straight over a narrow lane then continue between fences and bushes for ½ mile, then keep ahead on a stony track that later becomes tarmac. You can access the car park through gaps in the hedge on the right or turn right when you reach the road through the village (or left to the station).

Spring

What to look out for –

Brimstone butterfly

The lovely brimstone butterfly is one of the first signs of spring and can sometimes be seen as early as February if the weather is mild. The male butterfly is a beautiful shade of yellow, and may even be the origin of the name butterfly, from 'butter-coloured fly'. The female is a paler lemon, the colour of the moon, and she lays her eggs on buckthorn. Both sexes have characteristic leaf-shaped wings, providing wonderful camouflage when they are resting or hibernating in clumps of ivy. It is the longest-lived of our butterflies and there is a second generation in summer, so it can be seen in most months of the year, often visiting flowers for their nectar.

2 Ightham Mote

The view from the Greensand Ridge towards the High Weald.

Starting at one of the loveliest moated houses in the country, this walk takes you through an undulating landscape on the Greensand Ridge, with fine views over the wooded countryside of the Weald. The middle section goes through the valley of the River Bourne, where you can see the remains of another historic house, the 13th century Old Soar Manor. There are also fruit orchards that are coated with blossom in spring and plantations of cobnuts. You return through woods full of spring flowers such as celandine, wood anemone and wood sorrel.

Spring

Distance 6½ miles.

Terrain An undulating route with some gradual climbs and several stiles.

Map OS Explorer 147 Sevenoaks & Tonbridge.

Starting point The car park at the National Trust property, Ightham Mote (GR 584536, TN15 0NU).

How to get there Ightham Mote is accessed from a minor road just south of the village of Ivy Hatch, reached from the A227 or A25 near Ightham.

Refreshments There is a restaurant at Ightham Mote. The Kentish Rifleman, ☎ 01732 810727, and Chaser, ☎ 1732 810360 pubs are passed on the walk.

The Walk

1 From the end of the car park furthest from the entrance, go to the left of the restaurant and through the staff car park to reach a road on a bend. Turn left on a stony track and after 500 yards, at a marker post, follow the track round to the left, rather than going straight on. Continue gradually uphill on the left side of a field, with a tall hedge on the left. On reaching a wood go straight ahead through a gateway and keep straight on at a marker post 50 yards in. The path goes through trees, with bluebells beneath, and later bends left, now on the left edge of a wood, to reach a wooden pedestrian gate to a road.

2 Cross the main road with great care and bear slightly to the right to go on a track at a bridleway sign. The track goes through trees then alongside a wire fence around a field on the left. Where the trees on the right end, look for a marker post on the right and turn left through a gap in the fence and diagonally right (1 o'clock) across a field, just to the right of a large oak tree. At the end of the field continue straight on through a gap in a fence and bank of trees, then ahead through an apple orchard. Continue alongside a tall hedge on the right, and between hedges then houses to reach a narrow lane opposite timbered cottages.

3 Turn left along the lane to soon pass an oast house on the left. After 20 yards turn right over a stile in the hedge. (To avoid a tall stile you could turn right on the lane at Point 3, then left at a junction to walk along a lane to Dux

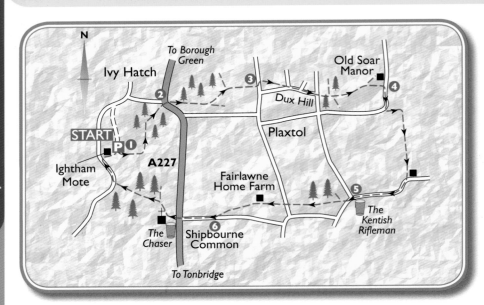

Hill.) Walk along the right edge of a field, with fine views ahead, to a stile in a fence to the left of a gate, then straight on towards houses. Go over a tall stile in a hedge to a road junction then go ahead to the right down **Dux Hill**. Keep straight on where a lane goes off to the left and when you reach a T-junction go straight over to a footpath sign by a wooden gate. Go ahead on a track alongside a wooden fence then through a small wood that is pungent with wild garlic in spring. Cross a footbridge over the narrow **River Bourne** then straight on along the right edge of a field, ignoring a stile on the right, to cross a shorter footbridge and go ahead over rough ground. At a marker post take the right fork and keep on the grassy path, soon with a tree-lined stream on the right and an old pear orchard on the left, to a stile by gates to a lane.

❹ (The walk continues to the right here but it is worth a short diversion of 300 yards to the left along the lane to view **Old Soar Manor**, a knight's house built in 1290. Then retrace your steps.) Go right along the lane, later passing **Broadfield Manor**, built in 1700, then as the lane bends sharp right, turn left along a dirt track. After 200 yards turn right through a gateway and along a track on the left side of a field, with trees on the left. There are cherries and later raspberries on the right and fine views. Go straight over a cross-track and keep straight ahead, later alongside a hedge around farm buildings and past a metal gate to a lane. Turn right along the lane, taking care around the bends. There are plantations of cobnuts behind the hedges and the lane later crosses the **River Bourne** and finally reaches a T-junction by the Kentish Rifleman inn.

5 Go left for 100 yards then up the bank on the right and through a kissing gate. Walk along the left edge of a field but after 100 yards go over a stile on the left and diagonally right (1 o'clock) across a field towards a wood. Enter the wood via a stile and go ahead through trees, with bluebells and other wild

The woods are carpeted with spring flowers, bringing colour before the leaves are on the trees.

flowers such as wood sorrel beneath. Leave the wood at a stile and go ahead across a field towards a gate in a gap in the hedge at the far end. Cross a stile with care onto the lane beyond and go straight across and along the drive opposite. Keep ahead to the left of farm buildings to continue on a dirt track past a wood, over a stream and across a field, then past gardens on the left and between more gardens to a lane.

6 Turn right and keep on this main lane, or on the grass alongside it, ignoring any side roads. Cross **Shipbourne Common** and reach a main road near The Chaser pub. Go straight across and into the churchyard then follow a path past the church to a gate. After 2 yards turn right over a stile in the hedge and go ahead across grass and between fenced trees, then alongside a hedge on the right. Cross two stiles in quick succession then continue ahead between wire fences to a stile 50 yards ahead. Go straight over a dirt track and past a yellow-painted post and up the left edge of a field, keeping right of the next yellow post 50 yards on to continue alongside trees on the left. At the next yellow post on the left bear right for 100 yards to another post on the edge of trees. Go over a stile and through a wood on a path between fences, then along the right edge of a field, through a gap in a hedge and along the left edge of the next field to a stile and a lane. Turn right for 100 yards then right again through gates to Ightham Mote. Go past the wonderful house, then left into the car park.

What to look out for –

Ightham Mote

The original moated house was built nearly 700 years ago but this late medieval house was remodelled in Tudor times. There are lovely views of the house over its moat, with fine stonework, timbered sections, mullioned windows and impressive chimneys.

The house is built around a large courtyard and inside there is a great hall and a Tudor chapel, dating from 1521, with a magnificent painted ceiling and window glass decorated with coats of arms. The National Trust has carried out extensive restoration work and has also created lovely gardens with pools, lawns and colourful flowers.

3 Pembury

A fine view to the North Downs.

There are superb views over the Weald of Kent from this walk through the rolling countryside around Pembury. This is a lovely undulating landscape with far-reaching views to the North Downs. The route takes you through fruit orchards that are covered with white and pink blossom in spring and woods that are colourful with wild flowers, or if you choose to do the walk in autumn, blazing with leaf colour.

Spring

The facts

Distance 4½ miles.

Terrain There are some gradual slopes and lots of stiles.

Map OS Explorer 136 High Weald, Royal Tunbridge Wells.

Starting point The village green at Pembury, off the High Street (GR 625407, TN2 4PA). Park around the green.

How to get there Pembury is close to the junction of the A21, A264 and A228, 2 miles east of Tunbridge Wells, with buses from that town.

Refreshments Pubs include the Camden Arms ☎ 01892 822012 and the Black Horse ☎ 01892 822141 or there is a nice café near the green called Nanna's ☎ 07874 004727.

The Walk

1 Cross the road with care to the Camden Arms Hotel and turn left, then after 30 yards go right into **Chalket Lane**, passing a church on the left. Continue along the lane as it crosses over the **A21** and later passes a sign for Howfield Farm and a derelict barn. When you reach a track going off to the right continue straight on for 30 yards then go left over a stile in the fence. The path crosses a buttercup meadow, going under telegraph wires and gradually uphill towards a ridge with trees. If the path isn't obvious aim for a gap in the trees about 400 yards to the right of phone masts. Look back for a great view over the Weald to Sussex. Cross a stile by a marker post and turn right on a track. After 100 yards go left at a marker post by a cross-track to walk alongside a wooden fence and cross a footbridge back over the **A21**. Continue straight ahead across a meadow, with far-reaching views to the North Downs, and reach a road.

2 Cross and turn right on the footpath alongside the road and continue ahead where roads later go off to the left, until you reach the junction with the **A21**. Here you go left up a bank at a fingerpost, 20 yards past the 'give way' sign. Go ahead along the right edge of a field then continue straight on at the far right corner. Continue over the right of a pair of stiles then after 10 yards take the left fork in the path to walk on the left side of a field. Near the end of the field take a left fork in the path to the corner of the field and go ahead through bracken and under holly bushes to a stile. Keep ahead across a field, with more fine views, and straight over a stony track to a path between fences that leads to

a junction of lanes.

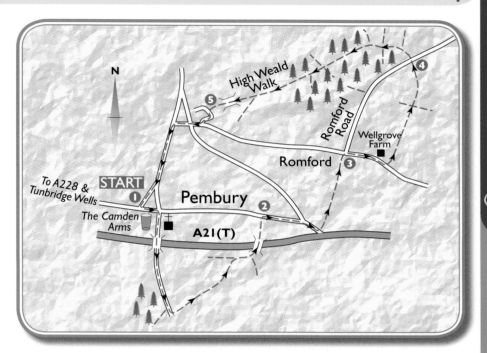

3 Turn sharp right. (To avoid several stiles you could go ahead along Romford Road for ½ mile and re-join the walk at Point 4 by turning left at the fingerpost for the **High Weald Walk**.) The lane goes gradually uphill to pass **Wellgrove Farm** on the left, then 30 yards after the entrance to stables go left over a stile hidden in the hedge. The path goes between wire fences and there are soon apple orchards on the right. Cross a stile and go ahead on the left side of an orchard to a stile by a gate and straight ahead to another. Continue ahead across paddocks via a succession of stiles, finally over one in front of a belt of trees then immediately over another on the left. Turn sharp right towards houses, passing another orchard. Cross a stile in a wooden fence and go ahead to the left of a white-boarded house and along a tarmac track to a lane.

4 Go straight across to a **High Weald Walk** fingerpost and a path on the left side of an orchard, with a wood on the left. About 50 yards before the end of the orchard turn left into the wood to follow a line of telegraph wires. Walk straight over a cross-track and downhill on a stony track. Pass a pumping station and 50 yards on, at a signpost, keep on the track as it swings left uphill. Keep ahead, ignoring any side paths, and keep straight on at a marker post with several arrows. The path soon goes between wire fences and bends left then right. At the next marker post on the left leave the High Weald Walk by going

Spring

The view near Pembury.

straight ahead, walking downhill between banks topped with wire fences. Cross a footbridge over a stream and continue between fences and under trees, then alongside a fence at the end of gardens.

5 Turn left at a marker post into a road on a housing estate. Go left alongside the road then turn right at a green with trees. At a T-junction turn right then at the next road junction go straight across and along **Romford Road** to a T-junction. Turn left to return to the village green.

What to look out for –

Orange-tip Butterfly

I always feel that spring has truly arrived when I see my first orange-tip butterfly of the year. Only the males have the vivid orange patches on the tips of the forewings and in April and May they can be seen patrolling along hedges and the sunny margins of woods as they search for a mate. The females have dark grey tips to the wings and lay their bright orange eggs on lady's smock and garlic mustard. Both sexes have a lovely mottled pattern on the undersides of the wings that looks greenish but is made up of yellow and black scales, and this provides fantastic camouflage when the butterfly is at rest on vegetation with its wings closed.

Teston Bridge Country Park

The medieval bridge at Teston.

This walk starts with a lovely riverside section alongside the Medway, with views of a picturesque medieval stone bridge and an impressive mansion. You can see waterside flowers, swans with their cygnets, and other water birds on the river – possibly even a kingfisher if you're lucky. Later the route winds through woods that are colourful with bluebells and other wild flowers and there are good views over the river valley. You also pass some lovely old churches.

Spring

The Facts

Distance 4¾ miles.

Terrain There are some gradual slopes on this route and the paths can be muddy at times.

Map OS Explorer 148 Maidstone & the Medway Towns.

Starting point The pay & display car park at Teston Country Park (GR 708533, ME18 5BX).

How to get there From the A26, 4 miles west of Maidstone, turn south on the B2163 to the car park. Buses (Arriva) from Maidstone and Tonbridge run along the A26.

Refreshments There are picnic tables at the country park, the Where Memories Meet tearoom in Wateringbury 1 mile west ☎ 01622 299017, the Tickled Trout pub at West Farleigh ½ mile south ☎ 01622 812589, and the North Pole pub 1 mile north ☎ 01622 812721.

The Walk

1 Walk out of the entrance to the car park, turn right alongside the road, and just before the bridge, cross with care and go over a stile. Walk along the bank of the **River Medway** for 1¼ miles, with views back to the medieval bridge. As you walk keep a lookout for birds such as swans, moorhens, coots and perhaps even a kingfisher. You will cross a few streams that run into the river.

2 When you reach a green metal footbridge across the river turn left away from the river on a narrow road that goes under a railway and climbs quite steeply up the side of the valley past attractive cottages. At the top of the hill turn left opposite a wooden barn along a lane leading to **Barming church**. About 30 yards before the entrance to the churchyard turn right at a footpath sign to go on a track across a field and reach the **A26**.

3 Cross with great care and turn left to walk on the road verge for 250 yards, then turn right on the road to **Hall Place Farm**. On reaching a corrugated metal barn turn left in front of it to go between farm buildings and through a metal gate, and continue ahead on a track. Keep straight ahead at a pylon to continue, with a wood on the right, and where the trees end go ahead for 150 yards on a grassy track to a marker post by a solitary hazel bush. Go ahead to the left of the bush on a grassy track that goes towards trees and gradually curves right, later

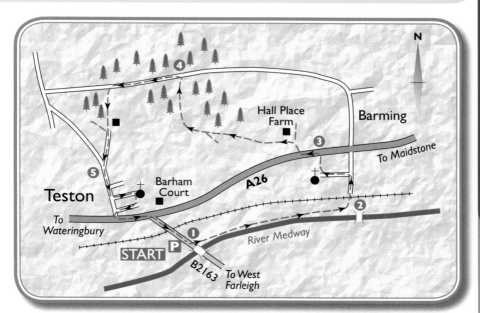

alongside trees on the right. Where the track swings left by a low wire fence go straight on into trees. The wide path goes uphill, with trees on both sides. Where the wide path swings left go straight ahead on a narrower path which goes uphill for 100 yards to a lane.

❹ Turn left along the lane, keeping aware of traffic. Pass houses on the right and after 300 yards look for a bridleway sign on the left of the road and turn left on an earth track. This goes downhill and has some large stones which can be slippery. Go past a large, partially thatched house and through a gate to a wide track on a bend. Keep straight ahead on this track, which soon passes more houses and becomes metalled.

A river scene at Teston Country Park.

5 At a T-junction with a road turn left into **Teston** village, taking great care as there is no footway for the first section. You will see a former cricket ball factory then by the post office and shop turn left along **Church Street**. At the end of the green area turn right alongside the churchyard fence to pass an information board and go on a path between a hedge and wall to reach a concrete road. Turn right and where this road ends bear left to the **A26**. Go left for a short distance and cross with care via a refuge then continue to the left on the opposite footpath for 300 yards. Turn right here alongside the **B2163**. As you turn it is worth looking to the left to view the lovely white mansion of Barham Court. Use the level crossing over the railway and turn right into the car park.

What to look out for –

Wood Anemones and Celandines

Walking through the woodland section of this walk in spring you will see lots of flowers that bloom before the leaves on the trees are fully open. They do this to take advantage of the sunlight before the trees cast a dense shade. Two of the loveliest flowers are the white wood anemone, sometimes called wind flower because of the way it moves in the slightest breeze, and the golden-coloured lesser celandine. These flowers attract insects such as bumble bees and bee-flies that are emerging from hibernation and seeking nectar.

⟳ 5 *Alkham*

A view along the Alkham Valley.

There is some wonderful scenery on this walk through the beautiful Alkham valley, designated as an Area of Outstanding Natural Beauty. In spring you can see some lovely wild flowers, when there are fine displays of cowslips, red campions, bluebells and wood anemones. You may even spot early purple orchids. There are glorious views over the valley and historic interest in the form of an ancient priory passed on the route and an interesting church in Alkham.

25

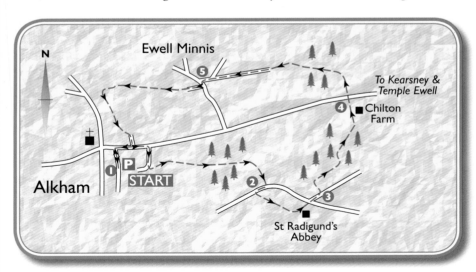

Spring

The Facts

Distance 5 miles.

Terrain Quite a strenuous walk with some climbs but only one stile.

Map OS Explorer 138 Dover, Folkestone & Hythe.

Starting point The car park in Hogbrook Hill Lane opposite (not at) the village hall at Alkham (GR 257423, CT15 7BX).

How to get there Alkham is 4 miles west of Dover and can be reached by a minor road from the A256 at Temple Ewell. Turn south into Hogbrook Hill Lane. There are infrequent buses from Dover and Folkestone (Stagecoach).

Refreshments The Marquis restaurant ☎ 01304 873410 is in Alkham and there are pubs in Kearsney and Temple Ewell, 2 miles east.

The Walk

❶ Walk back up to the main road, turn right for 300 yards alongside it, then go right along **Short Lane**. Where the lane bends right go left at a public bridleway sign along a rough track. Go through a metal gate and up the right edge of a field, with fine views along the Alkham valley on the left. Go through another

Wide open spaces are a feature of this walk.

gate and more steeply uphill towards a wood. In April look out for cowslips here. There is a view back to Alkham village. Go through a gate into the trees, full of wood anemones, celandines and violets in spring. At a fork by a marker post go to the right. On your left is a bank with trees and wild flowers such as red campion. Continue ahead between hedges and fields, then alongside a bluebell wood on the left. Take care as the path has large loose stones.

2 When you reach a lane turn right for 200 yards then go left over a stile in the fence at a footpath sign. Aim for a telegraph pole ahead, at 11 o'clock, and continue past the pole towards red-tiled roofs ahead. The path ends at a gateway. Go through it and on a path across a smaller field to reach a concrete road in front of the ruins of **St Radigund's Abbey**. Turn left on the road to reach a lane and go straight across and along **Minnis Lane**.

3 After 100 yards turn left at a footpath sign onto a track. At a cross-track turn right by an information board for **Gorsehill & Stonyhill Woods**, which contain rare orchids. Take the path sharp right, at 3 o'clock, not the one immediately right of the board, and keep on the main path, soon with a wire fence on the left and later with fields visible through trees on the right. Ignore paths going left into the woods and keep on the path alongside the wire fence around fields on the right. After ¼ mile this path swings left into the wood and curves right and downhill under trees. Go ahead past another information board to a wooden pedestrian gate out of the wood. Turn right on a cross-path and after 100 yards go through a metal gate and down the left side of a field towards farm buildings. Go through two more gates and on a rough road through the farm to reach a main road.

4 Go straight across with care and up a rough track to reach a wider track on a bend. Turn left on this track and don't stray from it as the area is used for military training. The track goes gradually uphill, with good views ahead along the valley and colourful downland flowers alongside. It then goes into trees where you may see early purple orchids on the bank on the right. Continue alongside a field on the right. The track bends left, now between wire fences and fields, and becomes a tarmac road near farm buildings. At a T-junction turn left for 200 yards.

5 At the next T-junction by a phone box and signpost go left for 10 yards then right along **Green Lane**. Keep on this lane, which later becomes a track and gradually bends left. After passing isolated cottages it becomes a narrower path. Go through a gate and ahead along the side of the hill, with views of Alkham church and the village below. Go through a metal gate and follow a path then a lane downhill. You reach the main road opposite the recreation ground. Turn right to find a safer place to cross back to the car park.

What to look out for –

St Radigund's Abbey

St Radigund's Abbey was built in 1191 and was occupied by monks from France. Its wealth and reputation increased in the early years. In 1302 Edward I received the great seal here and delivered it to William Greenfield, his Chancellor at the time. However, the buildings gradually fell into disrepair and the monastery was dissolved in 1538. Fortunately, some of the buildings have survived and the remains of the gatehouse, nave, transept, chapter house and refectory provide a picturesque and atmospheric scene. Inside the church at Alkham is a coffin lid bearing one of the oldest inscriptions in Kent. It came from the coffin of Herbert de Averenches, a monk at St Radigund's.

6 Chiddingstone Causeway

Kent oast houses were designed for drying hops as part of the brewing process.

This is a pleasant walk through typical Wealden countryside of woods, ponds and fields edged with hedgerows. In these hedges you can see the colourful and fragrant flowers of summer, such as wild rose and honeysuckle, and watch gatekeeper and meadow brown butterflies visiting the bramble blossom. Some of the hedges have wild hops twining through them and, together with the converted oast houses you pass on the walk, provide a reminder of the time when hop growing was an important activity here. However today, most of the fields are used for growing other crops or grazing animals.

Summer

Summer

The Facts

> **Distance** 4 miles.
>
> **Terrain** Fairly level but field paths can be very muddy after wet weather due to the clay soils; several stiles and some steps.
>
> **Map** OS Explorer 147 Sevenoaks & Tonbridge.
>
> **Starting point** A lay-by in Chiddingstone Causeway near the post office and opposite the Causeway Hall (GR 517466, TN11 8JR).
>
> **How to get there** The village is on the B2027, 5 miles west of Tonbridge. Penshurst station is close to the start of the walk.
>
> **Refreshments** Two pubs, the Little Brown Jug ☎ 01892 870318 and the Greyhound ☎ 01892 870275 are passed on the walk.

The Walk

1 From the lay-by cross the road and turn right on the pavement to walk past the **Causeway Hall**. Continue past the Little Brown Jug and the church then, opposite a road going off to the right, turn left at a footpath sign. The tarmac path goes between fields, with good views over the surrounding countryside, and reaches a lane.

2 Turn right along the lane for 200 yards then turn left on another lane, signed to **Charcott**. Where the lane bends right to the hamlet and the Greyhound go straight ahead on a rough track. After 100 yards turn right off the track through a pedestrian gate next to a wider one then go left in a long, thin field with a farm to the left. At the end of the field go through a kissing gate next to a wider gate then straight over a grassy track and ahead on the left side of a field alongside a hedge. Where the hedge ends keep ahead on a grassy track and through a gap in a hedge with trees. Continue ahead on a grassy track between fields then alongside a hedge that starts on the left. Go through a gap in a hedge across the track.

3 Immediately look for a marker post in the hedge on the left, and turn left through a gap in that hedge. The official path goes straight across a field to a gap in the tall hedge at the far end but if this path isn't obvious it may be easier to go right for 20 yards then left alongside a hedge and trees on your right and turn left for 40 yards at the end of the field to reach the gap. From the gap go straight across the next, smaller field to a gap in a wide hedge and a stile

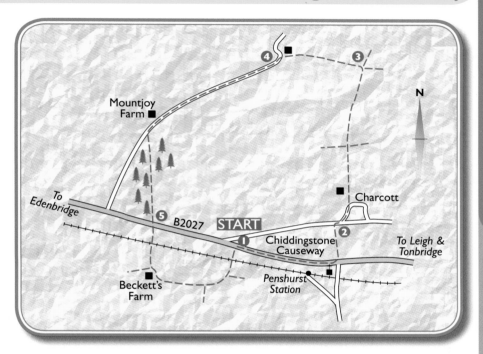

beyond. Go diagonally left (11 o'clock) across a field, aiming immediately left of a house whose roof is visible above trees at the far end of the field. As you get nearer, a tall marker post becomes visible – go past this and over a footbridge, with a pond on the right, then straight on over grass to a pedestrian gate to the left of a wider gate to a lane.

4 Turn left along the lane and ignore the first footpath sign on the left after ¼ mile to continue on the lane for another ½ mile. Pass the entrance to **Mountjoy Farm** then after 200 yards turn left at a footpath sign to go over a footbridge and through a black pedestrian gate. Go diagonally right (2 o'clock) across a small field to a gate into a wood and on a path through trees, soon bending left. Go straight over a cross-track and ahead to the left of a long pond and continue straight on, ignoring any side paths. You pass several more ponds as you continue through the wood to reach a busy road.

5 Cross with great care to a track to the left of **Carbery Cottage**, leading to **Beckett's Farm**. Cross a bridge over a railway and just before the farmyard and a converted oast house go over a stile in the fence on the left. Turn right to walk behind the garden of the oast house and past a small oak tree to go over a stile in the corner of a hedge. Cross a footbridge then go ahead to reach a line

Summer

of trees on the right. Continue ahead alongside them on the right edge of the field. Ignore a stile on the right and continue for 100 yards to a stile to the right of a metal gate then go ahead for 100 yards in a smaller field to a gap in a hedge. Turn sharp left here on the left edge of a field alongside a tall hedge. At a short marker post in the hedge keep straight on (the path to the right goes to the station) to a stile and steps up a railway embankment. Cross the railway with care and go down the steps to a stile and ahead on the left side of a sports field to the lay-by.

Wild roses in the hedgerows.

What to look out for –

Gatekeeper Butterfly

The pretty orange and brown gatekeeper butterfly is sometimes called the hedge brown and both of these names are apt as it can be seen flying around hedgerows and gateways in midsummer. It often visits bramble blossoms and other flowers such as thistles and knapweeds and can also be seen basking on leaves with wings fully open. The eye-spots on the wings are probably designed to distract birds into pecking at that part of the wing, rather than at the vulnerable head or body. The caterpillars feed on various grasses and hibernate when quite small, resuming feeding in the spring.

7 Horton Kirby

The river Darent at Horton Kirby.

Walking alongside the clear waters of the River Darent you can see colourful dragonflies and damselflies darting around and landing on the bankside vegetation, which includes wild yellow irises. There are water birds such as coots and moorhens, and even the occasional kingfisher. The water is clear enough to spot fish swimming around. There are lovely views along the river and across the lakes and you will also see an historic church and an impressive railway viaduct. This feat of Victorian engineering towers over the countryside.

Distance 2½ miles.

Terrain This is a flat walk with no stiles.

Map OS Explorer 162 Greenwich & Gravesend.

Starting point On-road parking near the village hall and Environmental Studies Centre (GR 563693, DA4 9AX) or in the car park at Westminster Field (GR 560685, DA4 9GR) from where you start the walk at Point 2.

How to get there Horton Kirby is reached by minor roads from the A20 near Farningham or the A225, 3 miles south of Dartford. Farningham Road station is ½ mile from the start.

Refreshments The Fighting Cocks pub is passed on the walk ☎ 01322 862299.

The Walk

1 From the village hall walk alongside the road towards the impressive railway viaduct that towers overhead. Just before the viaduct turn left by the Bridge pub to go for a short distance along **Station Road**. Immediately after crossing the river turn left at a fingerpost to go on a path alongside the River Darent, to follow a section of the **Darent Valley Path**. If you are walking in summer look out for dragonflies and damselflies, including the lovely banded demoiselle, with blue patches on the wings. There are also flowers such as yellow flag iris alongside the water. On the right is a large lake behind a metal fence. Keep straight ahead where there is a footbridge over the river on the left. The water is very clear and fish can be seen swimming around. Continue through a wooden barrier then along the left edge of a field.

2 You reach a red-painted building and the **Westminster Field car park**. In 1972 a granary and other Roman buildings were discovered here. Continue to the left of the building and ahead through the car park, then straight on for 30 yards to a wooden kissing gate, inscribed with Darent Valley Path, in the corner of the field. Go diagonally right (1 o'clock) on the main wide path across a meadow. Continue through a gap in the far right corner and ahead alongside a wire fence on the right. You are soon walking alongside the river again and continue under trees to a lane.

3 Turn left along the lane for 100 yards then go left at a fingerpost under

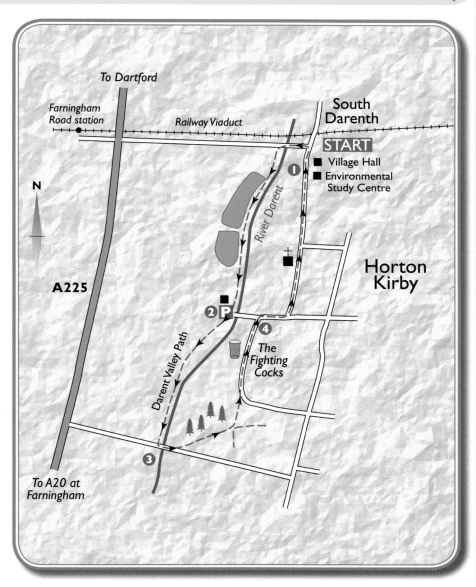

To Dartford

Farningham
Road station

Railway Viaduct

**South
Darenth**

START

■ Village Hall
■ Environmental
   Study Centre

River Darent

❶

N

A225

**Horton
Kirby**

✝

❷ P

❹

Darent Valley Path

The
Fighting
Cocks

❸

To A20 at
Farningham

trees to walk on a path between wire fences then ahead through a metal kissing gate. Where the path forks, 10 yards past the gate, take the left path alongside the hedge on the left side of a field to reach a lane. Walk ahead along the road, called **The Street**, soon reaching the **Fighting Cocks pub**, and also passing some interesting houses and flint cottages.

A restful spot on a hot day.

4 Follow the road as it bends right and continue around a left bend into **Horton Road**, ignoring the lane going straight on. Take care as there is no footway on this section. You pass the flint church and a hop garden on the left, then take the tarmac path that runs alongside the road on top of its right-hand bank. Where this path ends you are back at the start.

What to look out for –

Banded Demoiselle Damselfly

The banded demoiselle is one of Britain's loveliest damselflies. The males have dark blue patches on the wings and can be seen perched on waterside vegetation or flapping over streams and rivers, flashing blue. The male does a courtship dance in which he flutters in front of the female and will defend his territory vigorously. The females that they are trying to attract have lovely iridescent green bodies and lay their eggs in aquatic vegetation. Damselflies can be distinguished from dragonflies because they hold their wings above their body when at rest rather than holding them out at the sides like an aeroplane.

8 Sandhurst Cross

Looking over vineyards towards Bodiam Castle.

This walk crosses the county border into Sussex and goes through lovely undulating countryside, with the bonus of a fantastic view of the fairytale moated castle at Bodiam, with its turrets and drawbridge. Allow time to explore the castle before walking along the valley of the River Rother, perhaps going back in time as you spy a steam train on the restored Kent & East Sussex Railway. You will also pass hop gardens, a rare sight these days, and a vineyard.

Distance 5½ miles.

Terrain Undulating countryside with gradual slopes. Field paths can be muddy in wet weather.

Map OS Explorers 136 High Weald, and 125 Romney Marsh.

Starting point A car park at Sandhurst church at Sandhurst Cross (GR 791274, TN18 5NS). An alternative is to start the walk at Point 5. Park at Bodiam Castle which is free to National Trust members, check winter opening (GR 783254, TN32 5UA).

How to get there Sandhurst Cross and Bodiam are reached by turning south from the A268 at Sandhurst, 3 miles east of Hawkhurst. Infrequent buses from Hawkhurst and Hastings go through both villages.

Refreshments There is a tearoom at Bodiam Castle ☎ 01580 830196 and the Castle Inn nearby ☎ 01580 830330. In Sandhurst are the Swan pub ☎ 01580 850260 and Sandhurst Tearooms ☎ 01580 850181.

The Walk

① Walk back along the road away from the church to reach a crossroads and go straight across into **Silverden Lane**. Where this lane bends right go straight ahead on a tarmac track. Go past **Swallowhill House** but opposite its gateway, as the track bends left, go right at a footpath sign and up a bank to a stile. Continue across a field for 200 yards to reach the left end of trees and go straight on alongside them, then maintain direction across the rest of the field to go down steps under trees. Go over a footbridge then 5 yards on go sharp left through a gateway to a farm track.

② Go left on the track for 10 yards through a gap in a belt of trees then immediately right at a marker post to walk along the right side of a field with a tall hedge on your right. The field has paddocks then hops. At the end of the field turn right through a gap in trees and continue with trees and a stream on your left. After 100 yards turn left over a footbridge, thereby going from Kent into Sussex. Go diagonally right (1 o'clock) across a field then ahead through a gap between the end of a hedge and a wood. Follow a grassy track on the left side of the wood, then past trees on the left and ahead on a track towards brick buildings but 100 yards before them go left at a footpath sign.

Summer

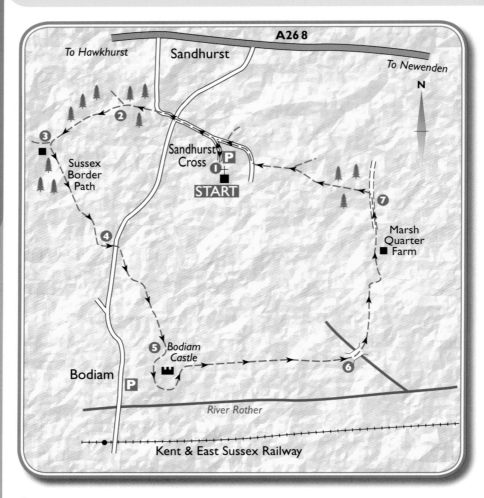

A268

To Hawkhurst

Sandhurst

To Newenden

N

② ③

Sussex
Border
Path

Sandhurst
Cross
① P

START

④

⑦

Marsh
Quarter
■ Farm

⑤ Bodiam
Castle

Bodiam
P

⑥

River Rother

Kent & East Sussex Railway

③ This grassy track is part of the **Sussex Border Path** and soon has a hedge on the left and later a wood on the right. Keep ahead under trees and over a stream to a stile, then ahead between hedges. Continue straight on where the path meets a stony track and as this track swings left past a metal barn go ahead through a kissing gate. Keep ahead on a narrow tarmac road, with more hops on the left and a view to Sandhurst church in the distance. Later the lane bends left to reach a busier road.

④ Cross with care to a gateway 20 yards to the right then go diagonally right (2 o'clock) across a field towards a large tree in a hedge. Go over a stile by the tree then sharp left for 100 yards to another stile. Keep ahead under trees for 40

Sandhurst windmill on the horizon.

yards then right up a bank to a stile in a fence. Go straight over a concrete track and across grass and an earth track to a marker arrow on the corner of a fence. Continue ahead on the right side of a field alongside a wire fence. Soon you have a wonderful view of **Bodiam Castle**. Where a hedge begins on the right, keep ahead on a path between it and one around a vineyard to reach the castle grounds.

5 The walk continues to the right of the castle and its moat then ahead to the left of a Second World War pillbox to reach a pale grey stony track. The route continues to the left here (the NT tearoom and shop are to the right) as you follow the track to a gateway with yellow marker arrow and go through a gate to the left of a cattle grid. (If coming from the castle car park follow the pale track running below the pillbox to the gate by the cattle grid.) Follow this track for a mile, later past a white-boarded cottage. You are walking along the Rother valley with the river some way to the right and beyond it you may see a steam train on the restored Kent & East Sussex Railway.

6 Go ahead up a bank by a pumping station and cross a footbridge over a drainage ditch, thereby re-entering Kent. Turn right along a bank for 20 yards then sharp left down the bank and ahead on an unmarked path on the right side of a ditch. After 200 yards cross a footbridge and go straight ahead up a field towards a pylon. Go through a pedestrian gate to the left of a metal gate and ahead past the pylon to a gate at the left corner of the garden of the house ahead. Continue ahead on a rough track past the house and follow it for almost ½ mile.

7 Look for the entrance to **Little Marsh Quarter** on the right but continue ahead on the track for 100 yards under trees, with a large pond beyond those on the left. As the trees end go left at a low concrete footpath sign on the left verge to go through a gap in a hedge and straight up a field to a wood that has a pylon at its left corner. Enter the wood at a stile then 5 yards on the path bends right then gradually left through trees to a gap in a fence. Go diagonally right (1 o'clock) across a field, aiming for a church in the distance. There are fine views over the Rother valley to the left and, behind to the right, Sandhurst windmill can be seen. Continue through a gap in a hedge then go diagonally right (2 o'clock) to a gate in a hedge. Go diagonally left across a field towards the church and over a stile to a tarmac road. Turn right along the road to a T-junction then left to the church (or right if you need to return to Bodiam).

What to look out for –

Bodiam Castle

Bodiam Castle was built in 1385 in a defensive position on the River Rother because the area was thought to be vulnerable to attack by French ships sailing up the river. The exterior walls with their battlements and turrets are virtually complete, creating a wonderful  sight as they tower over the moat. The moat is very wide, so creating a good defensive barrier, and would have been crossed by drawbridges that could be raised if it was under attack. There was further protection in the form of portcullises, one of which still survives, and murder holes, through which objects could be dropped on attackers.

9 Bredgar

The gabled porch of Bexon Manor.

Starting at the picturesque village of Bredgar, with its large duck pond, fine church and lovely timbered houses, this walk on the top of the North Downs has distant views over the Swale estuary to the Isle of Sheppey and Essex beyond. The route uses field paths and quiet lanes, where some of the verges have colourful wild flowers in summer. You also pass some interesting old cottages.

43

Distance 4½ miles

Terrain A mainly flat walk but with several stiles.

Map OS Explorer 148 Maidstone & the Medway Towns.

Starting point In Bexon Lane at parking spaces opposite the church or at the village hall (GR 880603, ME9 8EX).

How to get there Bredgar is 2 miles south-west of Sittingbourne, reached by minor roads from the A2 or A249. At the village church turn east into Bexon Lane.

Refreshments The Sun Inn ☎ 01622 884221 and the café at Bredgar Farm Shop ☎ 01622 884423 are both in the village.

The Walk

❶ If you parked near the church continue down **Bexon Lane** past the school then go up steps on the right at a footpath sign. (If you parked at the village hall turn right from the exit for 20 yards then left up steps at the sign.) At the top of the steps and with your back to the lane go diagonally left (10 o'clock) across a

The base of Bredgar Church tower is part of an earlier Saxon church.

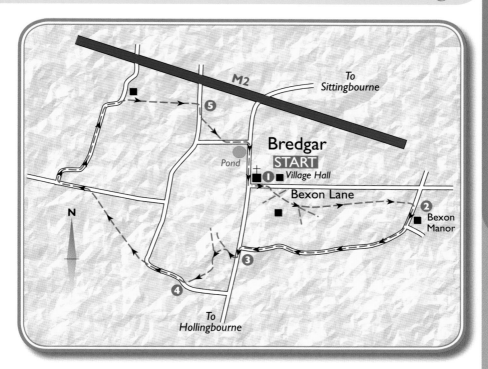

field, aiming for the left edge of a tall hedge at the far side. At the corner of the hedge the path splits into three. Take the left-hand path, aiming for the end of a hedge that projects out into the field 300 yards ahead. Continue alongside the hedge, then ahead under telephone wires to the corner of another hedge. Keep ahead then straight on across a smaller field and finally over a lawn via kissing gates to reach a lane.

2 Turn right, soon passing a lovely brick and thatch cottage and an oast house. Later you pass the timbered **Bexon Manor**. The house, with its intricately carved porch, dates from the early 17th century. Keep straight on along the lane, soon bending right. Continue along the lane for ¾ mile, with far-reaching views on the right to the Swale estuary, Isle of Sheppey and Essex beyond.

3 At a T-junction with a busier road turn left with care for 30 yards then, just before the drive to 'Westfield' go right through a gap in the hedge by a footpath sign. Go diagonally right (2 o'clock) across the field but at a crossroads of paths after 200 yards go sharp left on the cross path, aiming for the right corner of the horse paddock on the left. Keep straight on alongside the hedge at the end of the paddock and where the hedge ends take the right fork in the path to reach **Blind Mary's Lane**.

4 Turn right along the lane, soon with good views on the right, but where it bends sharply to the right go straight on at a footpath sign. Go diagonally right (1 o'clock) across a very long field, aiming about 200 yards right of red-roofed houses with trees behind. On reaching a lane, turn left. After passing two houses on the left, turn right into another lane. This lane soon bends sharp right then left. On its verge in high summer are colourful flowers such as lilac scabious, yellow St John's wort and agrimony, white bladder campion and bedstraw, and bright pink mallow. Later the lane bends right past an electricity pylon. Shortly after it bends to the left go right at a footpath sign by a flint wall. Go over a stile next to a gate and ahead on a track past a barn, then on the left side of a field. Go through another gate and along the left edge of another field, with Bredgar church visible ahead. Where the hedge on the left ends keep straight on, soon on a rough track to the right of farm buildings and past tall metal gates to a lane.

5 Turn right for 40 yards then left through a gap in a tall hedge at a footpath sign. Go diagonally right (2 o'clock) across a field, aiming for the church tower visible behind trees. Continue through a kissing gate in a fence and cross a recreation ground to its far left corner. Turn left alongside a road to reach the main road through the village by the large pond. Turn right alongside the road, passing the 14th-century Chantry House and some other lovely old houses then cross to go through the churchyard to the car park.

What to look out for –

Bladder Campion

Bladder campion can be recognised by the large 'bladders' behind the white flowers, which have deeply divided petals. The flowers look similar to those of its close relation the white campion but that species lacks the bladder. Bladder campion can grow to a height of over 2½ ft and is fairly common on roadside verges, particularly on the chalk soils of the downs. The flowers release scent at dusk to attract the moths that pollinate them.

10 Wingham

Timber-framed houses in Wingham.

Historic houses and churches are features of this walk **through** pleasant countryside between Canterbury and Sandwich. You also pass thatched cottages and a restored windmill at Chillenden, while a short diversion will take you to the lovely gardens at Goodnestone House. The walk starts at the village of Wingham, which has several attractive timbered houses and an impressive church, with a steeple that can be seen for miles.

47

Summer

The Facts

Distance 6½ miles.

Terrain Mainly flat, some field paths could be muddy after rain, a few stiles.

Map OS Explorer 150 Canterbury & the Isle of Thanet.

Starting point The public car park in Wingham (GR 244576, CT3 1DW).

How to get there Wingham is 6 miles east of Canterbury. Turn off the A257 opposite the Anchor Inn into the car park. There are regular buses (Stagecoach) from Canterbury and Sandwich.

Refreshments In Wingham, there's the Dog Inn ☎ 01227 720339 and the Anchor Inn ☎ 01227 720229. The Fitzwalter Arms in Goodnestone is passed on the walk ☎ 01304 840303.

The Walk

❶ From the car park turn left alongside the main road and as it bends right go left on a tarmac track alongside a bank. Go between houses then straight ahead on a narrower path that bends right to reach a suburban road. Turn left and at the end of the cul-de-sac take a path in the right corner for 30 yards then go sharp right before new houses on an unmarked path alongside a brick wall then between garden fences to a road.

❷ Turn left along the road, taking care as there is no footway. After ¼ mile, where the road bends right, go straight ahead along a tarmac track to the left of a sign for Brook Farm. Keep on this farm road for 1 mile, passing the entrance to **Brook Farm**, and continue to where the road swings left through a wide gap in the hedge. Here go straight ahead on a stony track alongside a hedge on the left, then after 250 yards go right at a T-junction with a narrow tarmac road. After 250 yards go left at a footpath fingerpost on a grassy track with a tall hedge on the right, and 50 yards before telephone wires turn right through a gap in this hedge onto a path between fences. The path becomes a stony track and you pass the church at **Staple**. Take care as you step out into a road.

❸ Turn left alongside the road past the church then, where the main road bends left, go ahead along a narrow lane. Keep right where it forks after 150 yards to pass a thatched cottage. Stay on the lane for ½ mile until you reach a

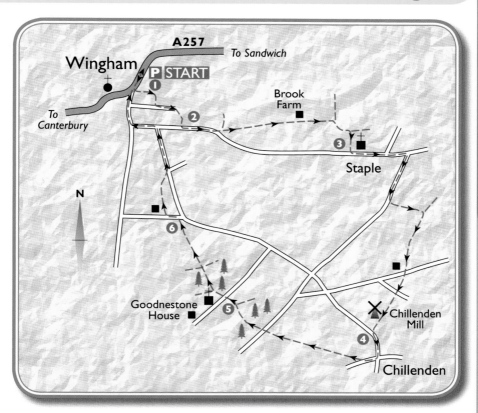

footpath fingerpost on the left. Go left here on a grassy track between fields and later alongside a privet hedge. Where the track and hedge bend left, go sharp right on a grassy track between fields. Continue past the left end of a hedge towards another hedge, with an open barn visible beyond. Go straight ahead through a narrow belt of trees and ahead across a field, aiming for the left edge of a row of tall trees at the far end and 100 yards to the right of a Second World War pillbox. At a marker post by the trees go straight on for 50 yards to a lane and straight over to another path, now aiming for a windmill in the distance. Go straight across another lane towards the mill, then ahead over a smaller field, skirting the mill on its left side, and ahead on a stony track to a lane.

④ Turn left, and at a crossroads turn right. After 250 yards go right up the bank, at a fingerpost, to a kissing gate then diagonally left (10 o'clock) across a field, aiming for a solitary poplar tree at the far end. Go over a stile by the tree and straight ahead across a field towards a wood, passing under telephone wires. Continue straight over a lane to a path into trees by a fingerpost and ahead over a cross-track and under beech trees before leaving the wood at a stile. From here you can see the 18th-century mansion Goodnestone House and Goodnestone church tower. The path goes diagonally right towards houses, later bending slightly left to a concrete track that leads to the village street, with attractive cottages and the Fitzwalter Arms to the left. A slightly longer diversion to the left (400 yards each way) takes you to the lovely gardens and tearoom at Goodnestone House.

5 The walk continues by going straight across the village street and along another concrete track. Go straight over a cross-track then 40 yards on go through a gap in a hedge then diagonally right (2 o'clock) across a field for 200 yards.

St Mary's steeple at Wingham is a much-loved landmark.

Continue alongside a tall hedge on the right, with trees behind, and where this ends go straight over a grassy track then diagonally left (10 o'clock) across a field towards trees. Enter the romantically named **Loverswalk Wood** past a marker post to walk under trees for 100 yards then keep ahead (not to the left) on a grassy track alongside a wire fence. Continue ahead, with Wingham church steeple visible in the far distance, to reach a lane by a thatched cottage.

6 You have the option of returning to Wingham by going straight ahead along the lane opposite, thereby avoiding some fields where there may be horses.

Alternatively, to avoid more road walking, turn left down Crockshard Hill and opposite a converted oast on the left turn right into the drive of **Crockshard Farm**. After 20 yards go right through a gateway and maintain your previous direction alongside a hedge on the left for 100 yards to a metal kissing gate in a fence. Keep ahead across the next small field past goats and ponies to another gate by pig sties, then ahead to a gate in the far left corner of the next field. Continue along the left edge of the next two fields then across a smaller field to a kissing gate and a lane. Turn left along the lane (ignoring another lane going off ahead) and go past a recreation ground. At a T-junction turn left for 300 yards then go right at a T-junction with a busier road. You soon reach the main road through **Wingham** and keep straight on to reach the car park.

What to look out for –

Chillenden Windmill

The trestle-post windmill at Chillenden was built in 1868, the last post mill to be built in Kent, and replaced an earlier mill that had blown down. It occupies a prominent position in the countryside, making a lovely sight with the white mill and sails set against a blue sky. It was a working mill until 1949 when it lost a sail in a gale, but has been restored by Kent County Council and is open to the public on Sunday afternoons in summer.

11 Mereworth

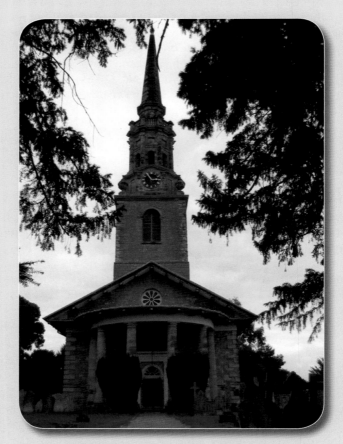

The Palladian-style St Lawrence's Church at Mereworth.

Starting in the village of Mereworth, near the classic Palladian-style church with its eye-catching steeple and remarkable neo-classical interior, this route takes you past a cobnut plantation and fields where strawberries and other soft fruit are grown. You pass a large pond with ducks then a section through woodland that displays a lovely palette of leaf colours in the autumn sunshine. The woods are filled with birds, the large nests of wood ants and many toadstools. There are also fine views on the walk and you pass an attractive 17th century mansion.

The Facts

Autumn

Distance 4 miles.

Terrain A walk with some gradual slopes. Some paths can be muddy.

Map OS Explorer 148 Maidstone & the Medway Towns.

Starting point The lay-by near the church in Mereworth (GR 660537, ME18 5LY).

How to get there Mereworth is 6 miles west of Maidstone, at the junction of the A26 with the A228. Buses (Arriva) from Maidstone, Tonbridge and Kings Hill run through the village.

Refreshments The Moody Mare gastropub is on the B2016 about ¾ mile north-west of Mereworth ☎ 01622 813038, and the Swan is in West Peckham, 1 mile west ☎ 01622 812271. There is also a good selection of pubs and cafés in West Malling, 2 miles north.

The Walk

1 At the end of the lay-by nearest the church look for a footpath sign on the verge and cross the road to go on a tarmac track alongside **Torrington House**, walking between houses then ahead on a path to the left of a cottage. Behind the hedge on the right of the path is a plantation of cobnuts. After 200 yards, where the path divides, keep right on a path between a hedge on the left and fence on the right, to reach a stile and go ahead on a drive until you reach a lane. Keep straight on along the lane, which soon bends left, and keep left where it forks, passing a large house and with good views to the left later. Continue straight on where **New Pound Lane** goes off to the right and past a thatched barn to reach a main road.

2 Cross the busy road with great care and go along a track at a footpath fingerpost. Soon pass a metal gate (signed No Bridleway) and go ahead on the left side of a field. Lots of strawberries are grown here, many on a table-top system under plastic tunnels. Keep right at a fork in the track and continue straight on to go past a metal gate to a lane.

3 Turn left along the lane for 100 yards then turn right, immediately after a large pond, to go on a track alongside the pond. Continue ahead to the right of a stone cottage then left of a line of conifer trees and through a gate in a metal barrier. Keep straight on along a path on the left side of a valley. Where

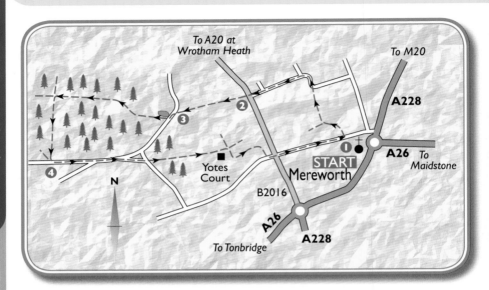

the path reaches trees don't enter the wood but veer right alongside the trees, soon bending left to walk through an open area that gradually narrows, with trees on both sides. The path enters the wood, going gradually uphill between tall conifer trees then on a track between hazel bushes. After ½ mile you reach a crossroads of tracks near a group of oak trees (no markers). Go left here on a track that climbs gradually uphill between low banks. Look out for the large nests of wood ants, made of pine needles and other debris. Keep straight on where a track comes in from the left and continue ahead for ½ mile on a track between trees that are coppiced (cut down to ground level) every few years. You may also see fly agaric toadstools, crimson with white spots – attractive but poisonous.

4 On reaching a lane by a metal barrier turn left along the lane. Keep straight on where **Peckham Hurst Road** comes in from the right then, just past the drive to The Hurst, take the right fork in the lane. At a T-junction with another lane turn right for 30 yards then go left at a wooden fingerpost onto a track through trees. Keep straight ahead to the right of a fenced area with a telephone mast disguised as a tree. There are fine views to the right as you go downhill and the mansion of Mereworth Castle, with its distinctive dome, can be seen in the distance. Go straight ahead at a cross-track to keep left of a house and later over another cross-track and ahead on a wide track between wire fences. There are good views of the back of **Yotes Court**, a 17th-century mansion, on the right. At a T-junction with another track turn right, on a drive past houses. Immediately after Yotes Cottage, with its unusual arched windows, turn left on

Autumn colours in the woods.

a track between a hedge and trees and past barns. Later the track bends right between trees and reaches a lane. Turn left for a few yards to the main road and cross via the refuge on the left then go ahead alongside the road through Mereworth village, past the school and on to the lay-by.

What to look out for –

Wood Ants' Nests

Wood ants make spectacular nests, up to 5ft high, using pine needles, twigs and leaf stalks. The actual nest, containing the queen ants and the larvae, is underground, while the mound of debris protects it from the elements. The wood ant is one of the largest in Britain, up to 3/8 inch long, and is able to squirt formic acid as a defence mechanism. You can see trails of ants on foraging missions from the nest to find new nesting material and capture caterpillars and other insects for food.

12 Upper Halling

Autumn

Looking towards the Medway Bridge and Rochester.

This is an invigorating walk, with some climbs and descents on the North Downs, but you are rewarded with lovely views over the Medway valley, even as far as the historic buildings of Rochester. The countryside is very wooded, so looks fantastic in autumn as the leaves of the trees turn to bronze and gold and there are red berries and hips in the hedgerows. In the summer months, you can see lots of wild flowers, including orchids. The route passes close to a tiny Norman church and it only requires a short diversion to view this. Chatham dockyards are 6 miles away, considered by Dickens to be a 'place of wonderment'. The Historic Dockyard Chatham has buildings, museums and warships to explore. It also offers 'Dickens' Dockyard Tours' on Sundays in spring and summer. Check the website for prices and opening times (www.thedockyard.co.uk).

Autumn

The Facts

Distance 4¼ miles.

Terrain There are some steep climbs and descents and some of the paths can be slippery after rain.

Map OS Explorer 148 Maidstone & the Medway Towns.

Starting point On-street parking in Browndens Road, Upper Halling (GR 692639, ME2 1JH).

How to get there Upper Halling is reached by a minor road from the A228, 2 miles south of junction 2 of the M2. There are buses from Chatham (Nu-Venture).

Refreshments No refreshments are available in Upper Halling but there are two pubs in Halling, the New Bell ☎ 01634 240523 and the Homeward Bound ☎ 01634 240743.

The Walk

1 Walk back to the end of Browndens Road and turn left at the T-junction. After 200 yards turn right along **Chapel Lane**. Later there is a fine view on the right along the Medway valley to the Medway bridge, with Rochester castle and cathedral visible beyond. Continue on the lane as it bends left past a barrier and goes under trees, gradually becoming steeper.

2 After ½ mile follow the lane as it bends sharp right and becomes a rough track under trees. Keep straight ahead where there are gates on both sides of the track. After a further 300 yards, where there are black barriers and stiles on both sides, and markers for the **North Downs Way**, go over the stile on the left. After 5 yards turn right on a stony track between bushes to the edge of a field and straight ahead across it, going under power lines to the far corner (not the corner with a pylon). Continue past a marker post to a stile in a metal barrier and straight over a cross-track to a path going down through trees and dropping quite steeply to go past an isolated cottage and reach a narrow lane.

3 Turn left along the lane. Shortly after passing the drive to Winnats Farm go left on a track at a byway sign hidden in trees. Before you turn you may wish to view the tiny church of **Dode**, which is 200 yards along the lane, then return. The stony track passes between black barriers and soon bends right to go uphill, steeply at times. Keep straight on where a track joins from the left

Autumn

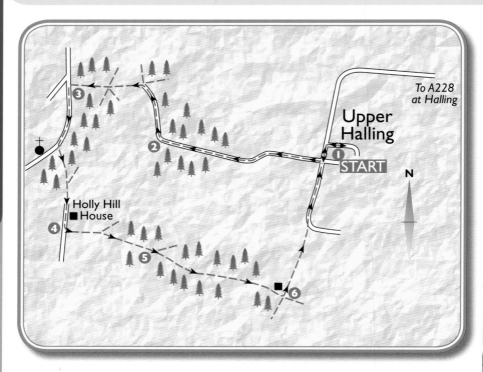

and walk alongside a wooden fence on the left. Continue past the wooden gates for **Holly Hill House** and a flint building.

4 At the end of the paling fence on the left go left at a fingerpost on a track between a fence and hedge, straight over a drive to the house, and past a metal gate. Continue ahead on the left edge of a field alongside a line of trees and keep ahead at a marker post after 100 yards, still on the left side of the field. At the end of the field turn left through a gap by a large ash tree then immediately right by a marker post to go through a gap (or over a stile) in a fence and ahead on a path through trees. The path later goes steeply downhill and can be slippery when wet.

5 At the bottom of the slope go through a metal pedestrian gate then turn left along a track for 20 yards then right through a wider metal gate by a marker post. As another path goes off to the left, go straight ahead on an earth track, to reach a cross-track after 300 yards. Go straight over and past a marker post on a grassy bank, where you can see orchids and other wild flowers in summer. The narrow path goes up into trees, soon bending left, right and left again, through beech, ash and yew trees, some with large trunks. Later the path goes under two sets of power lines and ahead past a marker post then downhill on a track between fences and past a white house to a stile.

6 Go sharp left on a stony track with a view ahead over the Medway valley. Follow the track between hedges and past a metal barrier then keep ahead on a narrow tarmac road. When you reach a wider road on a bend keep straight on to reach a crossroads, taking care on this stretch as there is no footway. Go straight ahead for 200 yards to **Browndens Road**.

Autumn

All that remains of the village of Dode, wiped out by the Black Death in 1349, is the deconsecrated Norman church.

Autumn

What to look out for –

Field Maple

One of the loveliest sights of autumn is the leaves of field maple glowing gold in the sunshine. It is one of our smaller trees and is often found in hedges. It likes chalky soils, so is common on the Downs. Unlike the related sycamore, it is native to Britain and the leaves are smaller and three-lobed. Both these trees have winged seeds, the familiar 'helicopters' that can travel some distance in the wind and so disperse the tree to new places. The wood of the field maple has a fine grain, so has been used for turnery and carving.

13 Lower Higham

Waterbirds at the RSPB Cliffe Pools nature reserve.

The atmospheric marshes of north Kent are the setting for this route, as you follow in the footsteps of Charles Dickens who often walked in this area. The churchyard of St James' church in Cooling is 4 miles from here. It was the inspiration for the opening chapters of *Great Expectations*. It is worth taking binoculars as the route leads through the RSPB nature reserve at Cliffe Pools, where there are many species of water-loving birds such as rare avocets. You can also scan the ships of various sizes on the River Thames and look across to Essex on the opposite bank. You will see historic forts, built in the mid-19th century to defend London from invasion along the Thames.

Distance 6 miles.

Terrain A flat walk but with lots of stiles.

Map OS Explorer 163 Gravesend & Rochester.

Starting point Roadside parking places near the church at Lower Higham (GR 716743, ME3 7LS) or alternatively in the car park of the RSPB reserve at Cliffe Pools (GR 722758, ME3 7SU) where the walk starts from Point 3.

How to get there Lower Higham is reached by a minor road from the A226 at Higham, then along Church Street. The RSPB car park is signed from the B2000 near Cliffe Woods.

Refreshments There are pubs on the A226 at Higham and in Cliffe.

The Walk

1 Continue up the lane past the church and where the road bends right go straight on through a pedestrian gate to the right of a metal gate then ahead on a stony path to the left of a converted barn. After 250 yards cross carefully over a railway line via gates then go diagonally right for 80 yards to a stile by a metal gate. From the stile go sharp right (3 o'clock) across a field, walking parallel to a double line of telegraph wires and 50 yards right of them. Cross a footbridge and continue ahead across the next field, walking halfway between telegraph wires and the railway line, to reach a stile in a fence and re-cross the railway. Go over another stile, ahead for 30 yards, then left over a ditch. You are now walking parallel to the railway, which is freight-only, and gradually veer back towards it to go through a metal gate (released by a chain on the left) and over a wooden bridge. Continue ahead alongside the railway to a stile and ahead to another in a fence. Go sharp left for 5 yards to a metal gate and turn right for 20 yards alongside the rails to a metalled road by a barrier.

2 Turn right on the road, later passing large metal gates via a gap on their left, and follow the road round bends to reach a T-junction. Turn left along this road, taking care on a bend, and continue past cottages. Where the road bends sharp right by a Tarmac works go ahead through gates on the access road to the **RSPB Cliffe Pools car park**.

3 Where the access road bends right go ahead through a barrier and along

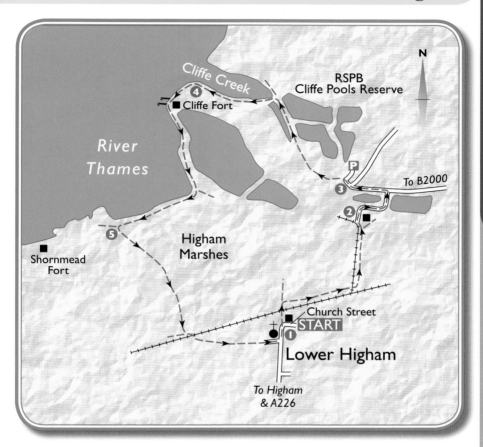

a stony track, or on the raised grassy bank on its left. Follow the track or bank as they bend right, then left, and continue straight on at the first footpath sign on the bank. At a second sign on the bank pointing right, turn left to go over a low wall via steps and ahead on a grassy path between muddy creeks, towards a gravel works in the distance. After 100 yards the path goes through a green metal gate in a barrier then curves right and left, with a creek on the right where you may see birds such as redshanks and little egrets. Continue ahead, now with a wall on the right and keep straight on where any paths go left into scrub.

4 At the end of the creek turn left to walk alongside the **River Thames**, with views of ships of various sizes. The path diverts left to go under a conveyor belt then continues between fences to regain the river bank. Soon you cross rusting metal rails via steps – the remains of a runway for the Brennan torpedo. As the bank and path bend left you can see the remains of **Cliffe Fort** on the left and

on the opposite bank of the river you can make out Coalhouse Fort. Keep on the raised path between the river and a gravel pit, with Gravesend visible in the distance along the river. Follow the grassy path, still alongside the river, as it veers away from the lake. Soon there is a taller grassy bank on the left, running parallel to the river. Walk along this higher bank until, near where a spit of land juts out into the river, there is a footpath board saying 'Circular Walks on Shorne and Higham Marshes'.

5 (The walk continues to the left here but if you want to see the remains of another fort at Shornmead, built in the 1870s, continue ahead for ½ mile then retrace your steps to this point). Turn left down the bank by the board and ahead for 200 yards to a stile by a metal gate then ahead on a grassy bank towards pylons, with a drainage ditch on the right. Go over a stile by a gate and continue ahead on a stony track under pylon wires, curving right to a stile by a metal gate with marker arrows. Go sharp left over a footbridge and ahead past a marker post and across a field to a stile in a fence. Cross the railway, then a stile, and follow the path as it bends left, parallel to the railway. Keep right where the path forks, to cross a footbridge, and keep ahead at a marker post. The path continues through scrub, with houses and a church steeple soon visible ahead. On reaching a rough road keep ahead past a thatched cottage to a T-junction and turn left to the church.

Looking across the River Thames to Essex.

What to look out for –

Cliffe Fort

Cliffe Fort was built in the 1860s as part of a defence system to prevent invasion of London by enemies using the Thames. Its guns could be used in conjunction with those of Coalhouse Fort on the opposite bank to set up an arc of fire over the river. In 1890 a Brennan torpedo, state of the art at the time, was based here. This early form of torpedo had two propellers that were rotated by wires attached to winding engines in the fort and could be steered. One of the launching rails can still be seen.

14 *Headcorn*

© Roger Miller

The river Beult flows through Headcorn and is a tributary of the river Medway.

The route begins by passing attractive timbered houses and the ancient church in Headcorn before crossing the River Beult and going through pleasant countryside south of the village. You walk on field paths, over streams and past small woods, which show some wonderful leaf hues in autumn. There are good views to the higher ground of the Greensand Ridge and you will often see small planes flying in and out of the nearby airfield.

Distance 4 miles.

Terrain The walk is mainly flat but there are lots of stiles and the field paths can be muddy after wet weather.

Map OS Explorer 137 Ashford.

Starting point The pay and display car park in Headcorn (GR 835442, TN27 9QQ).

How to get there Headcorn is on the A274 between Maidstone and Tenterden and is served by Arriva buses between those towns. Headcorn station is near the start.

Refreshments There are pubs and cafés in Headcorn, including the George & Dragon ☎ 01622 890239 and the Village Tearooms ☎ 01622 890682.

The Walk

1 Go out of the car park entrance and turn left along the main street through the village, passing some lovely timbered houses. Where the road bends right go straight on through the lychgate into the churchyard and follow the brick path towards the church. Opposite the porch turn left through a metal pedestrian gate to go on a stone-paved path past white-boarded cottages, then between fences. Cross the railway with great care as there are fast trains, then keep ahead between trees and over a footbridge across the **River Beult**. Continue ahead until the path ends at a stile on the right. Cross it and go diagonally right for 50 yards to a gap in a hedge near a double telegraph pole. Go ahead on the left edge of a field alongside a hedge to a stile and a lane.

2 Go straight across the lane to a gap next to a gate and ahead on the left side of a hedge. Where the hedge ends go left for 20 yards to cross a footbridge over a stream then ahead on the left edge of a field alongside trees. Follow the field edge as it curves right then left, with tall poplar trees on the left and an oast house behind them, until you reach a double stile. Go straight across a drive and between a garden and a garage, then turn left 10 yards past the garage to go through a gap in a hedge and over a stile. Turn sharp right along the field edge, by a wood on the right. Continue to where the wood ends, then go through a gap where a hedge meets the corner of the wood. Go ahead across a long field, walking about 30 yards to the right of a copse in the field and aiming

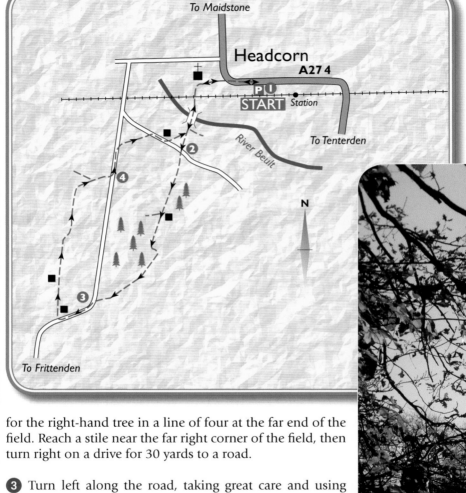

To Maidstone

Headcorn

A27 4

P U
START   Station

River Beult

To Tenterden

N

To Frittenden

for the right-hand tree in a line of four at the far end of the field. Reach a stile near the far right corner of the field, then turn right on a drive for 30 yards to a road.

③ Turn left along the road, taking great care and using the verge where necessary. After 400 yards pass a redbrick farmhouse with a green gate and turn right on the tarmac track that runs alongside it and past other farm buildings. At **Appleton Farm Oast** keep straight ahead on a rougher track and where this ends go through a metal gate and across a field to its far left corner. Go straight on here through a green gate (ignore another gate on the left) and ahead across a field towards an oak tree in front of other trees. As you walk there are views ahead on the left to the Greensand

Ridge. Continue past the tree and alongside a small wood to a stile in a wire fence and go ahead for 20 yards to another. Keep to the right edge of the next field, alongside a hedge, to a stile in the far right corner. Cross a footbridge and go diagonally right (2 o'clock) across a smaller field to a stile in a hedge. Turn right on a tarmac track to reach a road.

4 Go left along the road and just past the last house on the right, **Perrinwood House**, turn right at a footpath sign to go through a hedge, over a stile, and ahead across a field, aiming for the left of three tall oak trees at the far end (if the field is very muddy you could continue along the road and take the first lane on the right). About three-quarters of the way across the field you cross a

Autumn colours against a blue sky.

Autumn

footbridge over a wide stream and continue past a barrier and onto a lane. Turn right and 100 yards after passing **Forstal Farmhouse** turn left over a stile to the right of double gates. Go ahead across the field to a gap in the hedge to the left of a double telegraph pole then diagonally right for 50 yards to a stile in a hedge. From here you turn left on a paved path to retrace your outward journey over the river and railway to the churchyard and village.

What to look out for –

Timber-Framed Buildings

Headcorn has several superb timber-framed buildings on the High Street. Shakespeare House has massive timbers supporting a very high gable, while Chequers is a two-storey house under a hipped roof. There are other timber-framed houses around the churchyard. At the far end is Headcorn Manor, a Wealden hall house built as a parsonage around 1516, which has lovely oriel windows. The church also has some wonderful beams in the roof of the nave, making it one of the finest church roofs in Kent.

⟳(15) *High Halden*

The spiky cases of sweet chestnuts lie beneath the tree.

Starting at the village green at High Halden, near the lovely church with its unique timbered tower, the walk goes through pleasant rolling countryside with fine views. It makes for a great walk on a misty autumn day, as there are several sections of native woodland which are displaying their range of leaf colours at that season. It is also a lovely walk in spring and summer when there are woodland flowers to enjoy.

Autumn

Distance 4 miles.

Terrain An undulating walk with several stiles, some tall. The path can be muddy in places.

Map OS Explorer 137 Ashford.

Starting point The village green in High Halden (GR 901373, TN26 3LT).

How to get there High Halden is on the A28, 3 miles north of Tenterden. Turn south off the A28 opposite the Chequers inn into Church Hill, signposted to Woodchurch, and park near the village green. Buses from Ashford and Tenterden run through the village.

Refreshments The Chequers inn in High Halden ☎ 01233 850218 or a selection of pubs and tearooms in Tenterden.

The Walk

❶ Walk away from the main road along **Church Hill** then opposite the lychgate turn right on a tarmac path immediately before a school. The path goes alongside the school playing field to a kissing gate. Turn sharp left along the edge of the field for 50 yards then turn right, still alongside a hedge on the left. After 150 yards turn left through a gap in the hedge then go sharp right in a long, thin field, now with a hedge on the right. Go through a gap in a fence at the end of the field and ahead for 20 yards to a stile into a wood.

❷ Take the wide path going straight ahead, not the one going to the left. Walk through trees and straight across a cleared area under telegraph wires then follow the path ahead. When I last did this walk the route was marked by yellow tape on the tree trunks. After 100 yards the path bends left to a footbridge over a stream then goes diagonally right (2 o'clock) between oak trees to a stile in a wire fence. Maintain direction across the next field, later with a post and rail fence on the left, and go left through a wide metal gate in this fence. Turn sharp right alongside the fence and a pond and continue on the right edge of the field to a tall stile in a wire fence. Go diagonally left (10 o'clock) across a field, walking 50 yards to the left of a tree-fringed pond in the field, to reach a stile in a wire fence in front of trees.

❸ Go ahead between the trees, ignoring a stile and gateways on the left, and

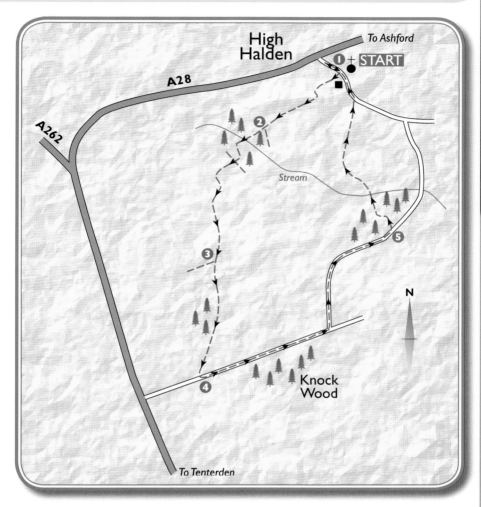

gradually downhill on the left side of a field alongside a tall hedge and trees. As you reach trees cross a low plank bridge on the left and continue ahead on the left edge of the wood alongside a wire fence for 200 yards to a tall stile. Continue ahead on the left edge of a field to a stile and footbridge then on a path through scrub and the fruit trees of a long-abandoned orchard. The path goes gradually uphill and can be slippery when wet. Keep straight on, ignoring any side paths, to go past a gate to a lane.

4 Turn left along the road, which is fairly quiet but take care because there is no footway. You continue on the lane past **Knock Wood** on the right then take the left fork into **Harbourne Lane**. Be careful around a right-hand bend and ignore the first footpath sign on the left. Continue ahead on the lane past a private road going off to the left. The lane goes under tall trees and past a row of cottages then enters a denser wood.

5 After 300 yards turn left at a footpath sign opposite a metal gate to go on a wide path through trees. Keep left where the path forks after 150 yards to reach a marker post. Turn left at the post, soon curving right for 150 yards to leave the wood at a stile. There is a seat on the left here if you wish to admire the view. Go ahead, slightly to the left (11 o'clock), down a field, with a white thatched cottage visible in the distance, and on a path into trees. Cross a footbridge and go through a pedestrian gate then sharp left for 10 yards to another. With your back to this gate go diagonally right (2 o'clock) up a field to a pedestrian gate in a wire fence. Continue straight on towards a large tree with a smaller tree to its right. Near the trees go ahead alongside a wire fence on the left to a footbridge and gate. Keep ahead on the left side of a field, keeping straight on at the corner of the hedge to go past the fence around a farmyard and oast to a stile and a lane. Turn left along the lane back to the village green.

What to look out for –

High Halden Church

The picturesque church at High Halden has a unique belfry tower constructed entirely of timber in the late 13th century. The tower is octagonal in parts and is braced by a system of massive oak pillars, beams and trusses – a tribute to the skills of medieval craftsmen. There is also a timber porch from the 14th century that has an entrance arch made with two halves of the massive trunk of an oak tree. Inside there is a 13th-century font and some stained glass.

(16) Faversham

Faversham Creek is rich in maritime history.

After walking along one of the finest medieval streets in the county, you pass some historic warehouses and continue alongside Faversham Creek, with its boatyards and restored sailing barges. You may see some of these barges and yachts along the creek. You can also look out for birds such as herons and little egrets as they search for fish. In winter, flocks of many different bird species, including the rare avocets, congregate near the mouth of the creek to feed on invertebrates in the mud, so it is worth taking binoculars. Later you can look across the Swale estuary to the Isle of Sheppey and Whitstable, and you pass a beach made up of shells.

75

Distance 7½ miles.

Terrain A long but flat walk with no stiles.

Map OS Explorer 149 Sittingbourne & Faversham.

Starting point The pay and display car park in Partridge Lane (GR 015615, ME13 7AX).

How to get there From the A2 near junction 6 of the M2 go north through Faversham to North Lane and just past the entrance to Morrisons supermarket on the left turn right into Partridge Lane, with the car park 150 yards on the right. Faversham station is ½ mile from the start and there are buses to Faversham from Canterbury, Maidstone and other towns.

Refreshments There is a selection of pubs and tearooms in Faversham.

The Walk

1 Turn right out of the entrance to the car park and where the lane bends right go straight on along a walkway between white-boarded houses. Turn left along **Court Street** and continue straight on along **Abbey Street**. This street has some lovely medieval houses, including Arden's House by the remains of a gatehouse to an abbey that was in this area. At the end of the street turn left to **Standard Quay** and follow the road round to the right, passing a late 17th-century warehouse with intricate brickwork. This now houses a tearoom among other things. On the creek to the left are restored sailing barges. At the end of a rough car park go ahead on a path in the right corner, walking between fences then past the converted Oyster Bay House. Keep ahead past boats in various stages of repair then cross a footbridge at the end of the boatyard.

2 Go straight ahead on a path near the creek, passing a water treatment works on your right. Look out for little egrets and herons fishing on the sides of the creek and some lovely saltmarsh plants growing on the banks, including sea aster, sea lavender and golden samphire. You may also see crabs in the shallow water. After ¾ mile turn left at a cycle track sign in front of a dyke to go on a grassy track alongside the ditch. Go through a kissing gate towards a house and straight on across a field to another kissing gate and a rough road.

3 Turn left along the road to pass houses, through another gate, and ahead on

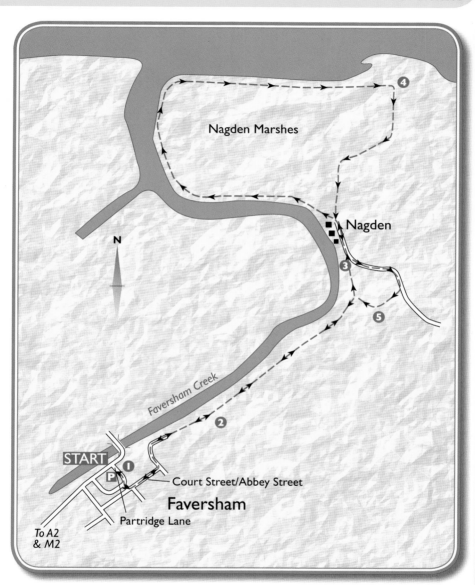

Nagden Marshes

N

Nagden

Faversham Creek

START

Court Street/Abbey Street

Faversham

Partridge Lane

To A2
& M2

a track past **Nagden Barn**. At the corner of the garden fence go left at a marker post to the bank of the creek, with a view back to Faversham church in the distance, with its distinctive spire. Turn right to walk alongside the creek. Just before reaching an electricity pylon the grassy track turns left through a kissing gate to enter Kent Wildlife Trust's **South Swale Nature Reserve**. Continue to

Faversham Creek was once filled with sailing barges bound for London.

the mouth of the creek where you can see birds such as the elegant avocet and redshank feeding on the mud at low tide and you can look across to the Isle of Sheppey. Go through a kissing gate and continue alongside the sea wall. After ¾ mile go through another gate and ahead towards a white beach, with Whitstable visible in the distance. Continue past the beach, which is made up of shells, and its lagoon, to where a wooden fence crosses the path.

4 Just before the fence turn right at a marker post by a kissing gate, to go down the bank, across a dyke, through another gate and straight across a track. Continue ahead on the left of a ditch towards a pylon. Go ahead at a marker post but at the next post, just before overhead wires, turn right over the ditch and ahead across a field, walking about 50 yards to the right of the left-hand pylon, to a fingerpost at the far end. Cross a dyke by the fingerpost and turn left on a rough track to return to **Nagden Barn**. Go straight ahead past the houses and continue along the rough road, following it as it bends right then 100 yards past the bend go right through a metal barrier at a cycle path sign in trees. Walk through the trees and between fences then cross a footbridge over a dyke.

5 Turn right for 30 yards to return to the path alongside **Faversham Creek** and turn left on it to retrace your steps back to Faversham. When you get back to Court Street you can return directly to the car park by turning right into the walkway between the Shepherd Neame brewery shop and a 'Simply Perfect' shop. However, to see more of the historic town continue along Court Street past the lovely Guildhall then turn right down **West Street**, which has more timbered houses. At its end turn right into **North Lane** and second right into **Partridge Lane**.

Winter

What to look out for –

Little Egret

Until the end of the 20th century the little egret was a rare sight in Britain but since then this elegant bird has become relatively common in southern England and now breeds in Kent. It stands about 2 ft high and is pure white with a long dark beak, long dark legs and with plumes on the head in the breeding season. It can be seen wading through shallow water as it searches for fish and shrimps, which it spears with its dagger-like beak. It looks impressive in flight, with its long legs trailing behind.

17 Chilham

A fine prospect over Godmersham Park.

There are many wonderful historic buildings to be seen on this walk through the stunning countryside of the North Downs. The route starts in Chilham, one of the prettiest villages in England, which has featured in many period dramas on screen and television. You then stroll through woodland on the top of the North Downs before descending through the lovely parkland of Godmersham Park. Here there is a glorious view over the 18th-century mansion and the Stour valley. The walk returns past black and white timbered houses, with a fine prospect of the Jacobean mansion of Chilham Castle over its lake, before ending in the village square surrounded by Tudor buildings. Surfaced paths make this a good walk for a winter's day and Chilham looks charming all year round.

Distance 4 miles.

Terrain There are some short but quite steep slopes on this walk and a few stiles. Much of the walk is on tarmac but there are also woodland and field paths.

Map OS Explorer 137 Ashford.

Starting point The car park on Taylors Hill, just off the A252 (GR 066536, CT4 8DD).

How to get there Chilham is 5 miles west of Canterbury, where the A252 joins the A28. Turn south off the A252, ½ mile west of this junction. Chilham station is ½ mile from the start and there are buses (Stagecoach) to the edge of the village from Canterbury and Ashford.

Refreshments There are two pubs in Chilham, the White Horse ☎ 01227 730355 and the Woolpack ☎ 01227 730351. Shelly's Tearoom is also in the village ☎ 01227 730303.

The Walk

1 Go out of the entrance to the car park and turn left past the fire station to walk alongside the **A252**. Continue past the village hall, which occupies a half-timbered tithe barn, and keep alongside the tree-lined road for ½ mile. Turn left into **Dane Street**, passing Dane Street House, which dates mainly from the early 18th century, and later a lovely timbered house on the right. Keep ahead as the lane becomes a rough track to pass **Woodpecker Farm** then keep straight on along a sunken track under trees, climbing gradually at first, then more steeply. Continue ahead where another path goes off right at a marker post. Be careful of loose stones on the path as you walk through the wood, with bluebells in spring. Keep ahead on the main track, ignoring any side tracks, to walk under tall beech, sweet chestnut and conifer trees. Take the left fork in the track by a large beech tree and 200 yards further on reach a cross-track on a bend by a gate.

2 Turn right on this track, which is part of the North Downs Way long-distance footpath, but leave it after 300 yards by going left at a marker post on the left, just before a sign for **Kings Wood**. Go over a stile in the wire fence near the remains of a deer leap, constructed to control the movement of deer. Go straight across a small field to another stile, with stunning views ahead across

Winter

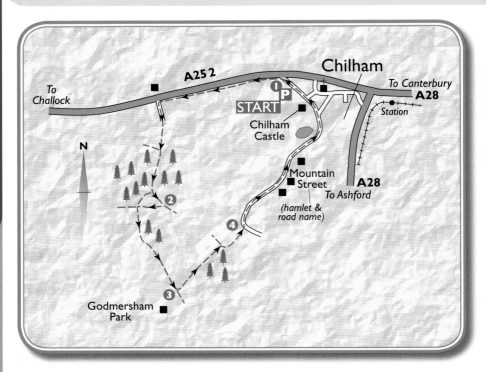

the Stour valley. As you continue downhill past marker posts there are views on the left to Canterbury Cathedral in the far distance. Keep ahead on a track to the right of trees to a stile in a fence by a gateway. The mansion of **Godmersham Park** is now visible ahead as you continue downhill on a stony track alongside a hedge on the left and past an attractive brick house.

3 Just past the end of the house's fence and driveway turn left on a rough track between hedges (no footpath sign). Continue ahead alongside a wood on the right, with arable fields on the left, and keep straight on to reach a wooden pedestrian gate to the left of a wider wooden gate. Keep ahead on a narrow track under trees, with good views on the right.

4 Go past a metal gate and ahead along a tarmac lane. Follow this lane for a mile, walking through the hamlet of **Mountain Street**. You pass two lovely black and white houses built in the late 15th century, Monckton Manor and Heron Manor, and later there are views of the house, lake and grounds of Chilham Castle. As the lane bends right turn left up the steep **School Hill** to reach the village square. Go left after the castle gates down Taylors Hill to the

car park.

Winter

Looking out over the Stour Valley.

What to look out for –

Godmersham Park

The Georgian mansion at Godmersham Park was built in 1732. From 1797-1852 it was owned by Edward Austen-Knight, the brother of Jane Austen. She would often visit him there and probably based some of the places in her novels on this area. Deer were introduced into the park in 1740 and the barn at Deer Lodge, identified by its clock tower, was used as a game larder. The lovely parkland has some fine old trees and great views along the Stour valley and to the hills of the Downs on both sides.

(18) Greatstone

Fishing boat off Dungeness.

This route provides a bracing walk by the sea to blow away the winter cobwebs. From this part of the coast at Romney Marsh there are great views over the bay to the white cliffs between Folkestone and Dover and to the shingle promontory at Dungeness in the other direction. You can walk along the beach, or on shingle and sandy paths. Look out for seabirds and shells, and jellyfish and other marine life swept up onto the beach. You can also see the small-scale steam trains on the Romney, Hythe & Dymchurch railway. The atmospheric landscape of Romney Marsh was used as a location for *Great Expectations* (2012), with the meeting of Pip and Magwitch filmed at the church in Fairfield.

The Facts

Winter

Distance 3¼ miles.

Terrain A flat walk on good surfaces, no stiles.

Map OS Explorer 125 Romney Marsh.

Starting point The pay and display car park at Greatstone-on-Sea (GR 082229, TN28 8ST).

How to get there Greatstone is on the coast road, reached by turning off the A259 at New Romney. Buses (Stagecoach) from Ashford and Folkestone pass the start.

Refreshments Several pubs and cafés are passed on the route, with others available in New Romney.

The Walk

❶ From the end of the car park nearest the toilets you can walk on a track over sand dunes and turn left to walk along the beach. However, to walk on a firmer surface, or at high tide, turn right from the car park entrance on the pavement alongside the road to pass the toilets. You could continue along the pavement all the way to Point 2 (1 mile) but for sea views turn right after 700 yards at a footpath fingerpost to go between houses called **Sea Wynds** and **Sea Leap** then 50 yards past the end of the gardens turn left on a sandy path. As you walk, there are views over the bay to the white cliffs at Folkestone and Dover and you can see plants such as sea kale and red valerian on the shingle, and gulls and waders on the beach. Continue ahead through the car park of a watersports club and past a lifeboat station then through a large car park behind houses and the Seahorse pub. At the end of the car park turn left towards the road then right past a white metal barrier on a shingle path which runs between beach huts and a grassy area with a playground. Continue on the path or on the grass until you reach wooden shelters near an information board for the Romney shore and a tall Victorian drinking fountain.

❷ Turn left here to go inland on the pavement alongside **Littlestone Road**, signed as the B2071 to New Romney and Dymchurch. Continue for ¾ mile alongside the tree-lined road until you reach a station for the Romney, Hythe & Dymchurch railway. Opposite the station turn left, immediately past the Captain Howey Hotel, along **Station Approach** by the railway. Continue ahead as the road becomes a concrete track and, where this bends left to a sewage

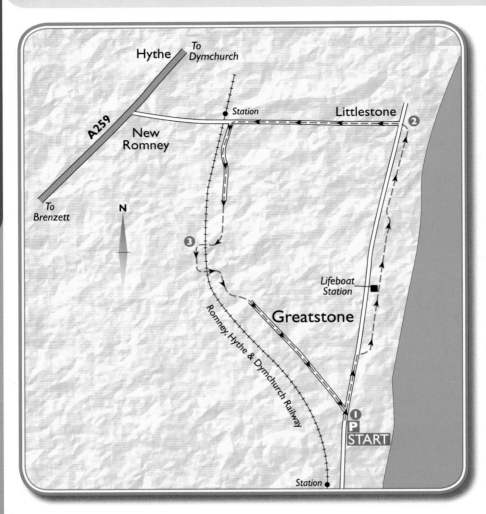

works, go straight on for 100 yards on a grassy track to a horse paddock. Turn right alongside the fence to cross the railway via gaps next to gates.

③ Go ahead for 10 yards then turn left at a mileage post to go on an earth track between hedges. Follow the track when it bends left after 200 yards, rather than going straight on. There is a view ahead to Dungeness power station in the distance. The track re-crosses the railway then you follow it as it bends through bushes. Ignore any side paths and continue until you reach a concrete road. Follow this road between houses for ¾ mile to reach a main road by shops, with the car park opposite.

The iconic white cliffs of Dover in the distance.

What to look out for –

Romney, Hythe & Dymchurch Railway

The Romney, Hythe & Dymchurch Railway was built in 1927 and runs for 13½ miles across the flat expanse of Romney Marsh from Hythe to Dungeness. It uses steam engines and carriages that are one third full size. The headquarters of the railway are at New Romney station, passed on the walk, and here there are engine sheds, a large model railway, buffet, gift shop and children's playground, as well as a 1940s museum (the museum is open April to September).

(19) Blean

The winding pond on the Crab & Winkle Way.

This walk is suitable for all times of year as it is entirely on good surfaces. You walk along part of the route of one of the first passenger railways in the world, the so-called Crab & Winkle Line that went from Canterbury to Whitstable. The line opened in 1830 and closed in 1952 but has been made into a cycle path. The pool that provided water to drive the steam engine, used to wind the cable to pull the early locomotives up the slope, is now a pond for wildlife. Winter provides the opportunity to appreciate the beauty of the structure of the trees in the extensive woodland and it is easier to spot woodland birds as they forage for berries, while the conifers provide some greenery. If you do the walk in June, you might see one of the rarest British butterflies, the lovely orange and black heath fritillary.

The Facts

Distance 5½ miles.

Terrain Mainly flat but with some gradual slopes, no stiles. The route is all on tarmac or shale surfaces.

Map OS Explorer 150 Canterbury & the Isle of Thanet.

Starting point On-road parking in School Lane in Blean (GR 123609, CT2 9HP).

How to get there Blean is 2 miles north-west of Canterbury. Turn off the A290 into Tyler Hill Road then turn left after the shops into School Lane and park along this road (not at the village hall). There are frequent buses (Stagecoach) along the A290 from Canterbury and Whitstable.

Refreshments The Royal Oak pub and family-friendly restaurant is on the A290 in Blean ☎ 01227 471247.

The Walk

1 Walk along **School Lane** away from Tyler Hill Road and at the end turn left into **Bourne Lodge Close**. At a T-junction turn right alongside a road (**Chapel Lane**) between houses and later tall hedges. Continue along the lane past large houses on the right, then 20 yards beyond some farm buildings, turn left on a tarmac track at a National Cycle Network sign.

2 Walk along this track, which soon has a shale surface, and beware of cyclists. The track bends left between hedges then past a conifer wood on the right. Soon there are trees on both sides and the track bends sharp right by a fingerpost sign. Look out for the large nests of wood ants, made from piles of conifer needles. There are also colourful flowers in summer and early autumn, such as yellow fleabane, purple knapweed, devil's-bit scabious and heather. After another ¼ mile you reach a stony cross-track.

3 Turn right here then follow the stony track as it soon bends sharp left. Continue on this track, ignoring any side tracks, for ½ mile until you reach a metal barrier and sign, just before a road at **Gypsy Corner**.

4 Turn left, 10 yards before the barrier, on a stony track through trees. After 300 yards there is a view to the sea through a gap in the trees on the right.

Winter

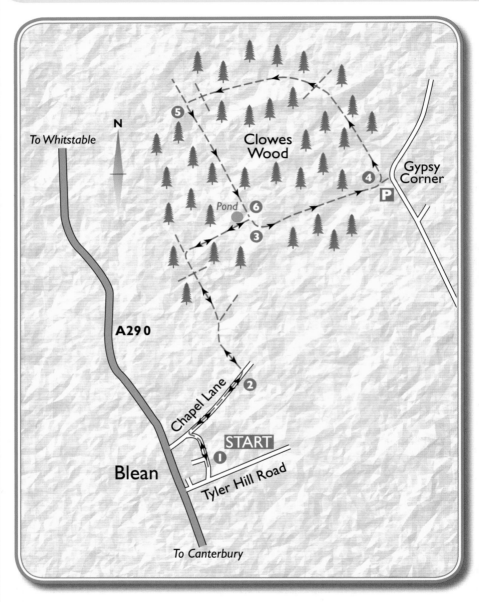

To Whitstable

N

Clowes
Wood

Gypsy
Corner

⑤

④ P

Pond ⑥

③

A290

Chapel Lane ②

START
①

Blean

Tyler Hill Road

To Canterbury

Keep ahead on the track and straight on past a marker post. The track is lined
by trees such as oak and lime, with conifers behind, and goes gradually uphill
then bends left and gradually down. Finally it goes uphill again and bends left
to reach a stony cross-track.

5 Turn left here, now back on the **Crab & Winkle Way**, and follow the trackbed of the Canterbury to Whitstable railway, which opened in 1830 and closed in 1952. You are walking through Clowes Wood and in June you may be lucky enough to see one of Britain's rarest butterflies, the lovely heath fritillary. After ¾ mile you reach a large pond hidden in trees on the right: this is the **Winding Pond**. The water was used by the static steam engines that hauled the passenger carriages up from the direction of Whitstable.

6 Just beyond the pond you turn sharp right on another track to retrace your steps back to the start. Follow the **Crab & Winkle Way** by turning left at a sharp bend, about 500 yards after turning right at the pool, and keep on the track until you reach **Chapel Lane** by the Cycle Network sign, then turn right along this lane. After 600 yards turn left into **Bourne Lodge Close** and **School Lane**.

Winter

Birds feast on the woodland fruits.

Winter

What to look out for –

Green Woodpecker

The green woodpecker is one of Britain's most colourful birds, with lovely shades of green on its back and wings, red on its head and a bright yellow rump that can be seen as it flies. It is often seen on the ground, as its favourite food is ants, which it catches with its long tongue. It survives almost exclusively on ants during the winter. It has a distinctive high, laughing call and this has led to two of its folk names being yaffle (hence Professor Yaffle in *Bagpuss*) and yarrow. The flight is very undulating and it can also be spotted on tree trunks, where it will make a nest hole in spring using its long, sharp beak. Male and female woodpeckers live separately during the winter, but stay in the nesting area.

20 Deal

Deal beach looking towards Ramsgate.

Here is a chance to experience sea breezes on a walk from Deal, with its narrow streets of cottages, many used by smugglers in the past. There are views across Sandwich Bay to the white cliffs of the Thanet coast as you walk alongside shingle beaches with their specialised plants. You can see birds such as gulls and turnstones prospecting for food. Later the sandy paths take you past gorse bushes and there are views across the sea to France as you return along the promenade to Deal. Here a short extension to the walk will take you to the historic Timeball Tower, a Victorian maritime Greenwich Mean Time signal, and Deal Castle.

Distance 4½ miles.

Terrain A flat walk, mainly on good surfaces, with no stiles.

Map OS Explorer 150 Canterbury & the Isle of Thanet.

Starting point The Middle Street pay and display car park in Deal (GR 377527, CT14 6HX).

How to get there Deal is reached via the A258. The railway station is ¼ mile from the start of the walk and there are buses (Stagecoach) to the town from Dover and Canterbury.

Refreshments There are many pubs and cafés in Deal.

The Walk

❶ From the **Middle Street car park** there are alleyways that lead to the seafront near the pier. Cross the road with care and turn left along the promenade to go past the **Royal Hotel**. Continue along the concrete path above the beach, with views over the shingle beach and sea on the right. On the left you can admire the varied architecture of the houses and cottages. Where the road on your left bends inland keep straight on along the promenade.

❷ Where the houses on the left end, continue ahead past an information board about Sandown Castle. This is the site of the castle, built in 1540 during the reign of Henry VIII as part of a chain of sea defences. Keep ahead on the raised shingle bank behind the beach or alternatively, if you want a firmer path with more shelter from the wind, on the path that runs parallel to the bank below its left side. As you walk there are views ahead to Ramsgate and Pegwell Bay and you can see the plants that have colonised the shingle, including sea beet and sea kale.

❸ After a mile look out for a sign on the left edge of the bank warning of the golf course. Continue for 100 yards then go left down the bank (no footpath sign) on a stony track. Go ahead on a path of sand and grass across the golf course towards the right end of buildings. Watch out for golf balls being hit across the path, which is paved in parts. At the end of the golf course go past a board advertising the Chequers restaurant, then a marker post. Continue alongside a wire fence on your right to reach a narrow road.

4 Turn left for 30 yards then go left through the car park of the **Chequers** to a grassy track that runs parallel to the road. You pass a brick pillbox from the Second World War and you may detect the smell of coconut, which emanates from the flowers of the numerous gorse bushes. When the track re-joins the road continue past a golf clubhouse then, just before houses, go left at a footpath sign on a path through vegetation. Most of the plants here are alexanders, thought to have been introduced by the Romans. The path goes behind gardens to reach the seafront at Point 2.

5 Turn right to retrace your steps back to the start, with views to Deal pier, and with the French coast visible on a clear day. When you regain the pier it is worth continuing ahead for 500 yards to view the Timeball Tower and Deal Castle.

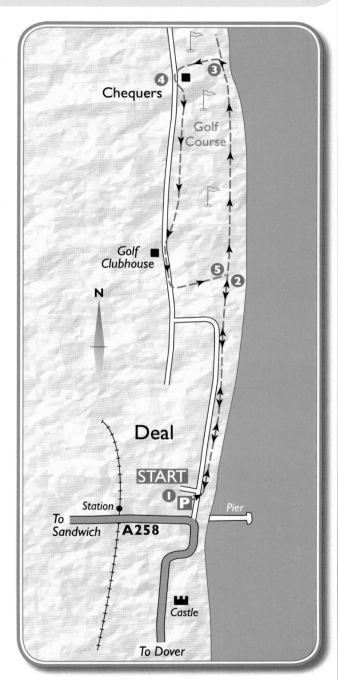

Winter

The sea front at Deal.

What to look out for –

Deal Castle

Deal Castle is one of a chain of Tudor artillery castles built around 1540 by order of King Henry VIII, who feared an invasion by European Catholic powers. The squat rounded bastions were designed to deflect incoming cannonballs and also acted as platforms for guns. Deal Castle guarded the sheltered anchorage between the shore and the hazardous Goodwin Sands. A short distance along the seafront is the Timeball Tower, now a museum. The iron ball on its roof was dropped at exactly 1 o'clock to warn ships to be ready to correct their chronometers.